FUNGI MEDIA
PERFORMING FUNGOSEXUAL MUTATIONS

Piotr Bockowski

The **MEDIA : ART : WRITE : NOW** series mobilises the medium of writing as a mode of critical enquiry and aesthetic expression. Its books capture the most original developments in technology-based arts and other forms of creative media: AI and computational arts, gaming, digital and post-digital productions, soft and wet media, interactive and participative arts, open platforms, photography, photomedia and, last but not least, amateur media practice. They convey the urgency of the project via their style, length and mode of engagement. In both length and tone, they sit somewhere between an extended essay and a monograph.

Series Editor: Joanna Zylinska

FUNGI MEDIA
PERFORMING FUNGOSEXUAL MUTATIONS

Piotr Bockowski

○
OPEN HUMANITIES PRESS

London 2024

First edition published by Open Humanities Press 2024
Copyright © 2024 Piotr Bockowski

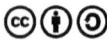

Freely available at:
http://openhumanitiespress.org/books/titles/fungi-media/

This is an open access book, licensed under Creative Commons By Attribution Share Alike license. Under this license, authors allow anyone to download, reuse, reprint, modify, distribute, and/or copy their work so long as the authors and source are cited and resulting derivative works are licensed under the same or similar license. No permission is required from the authors or the publisher. Statutory fair use and other rights are in no way affected by the above. Read more about the license at creativecommons.org/licenses/by-sa/4.0/

Cover Art, figures, and other media included with this book may be under different copyright restrictions.

Print ISBN 978-1-78542-139-6
PDF ISBN 978-1-78542-138-9

OPEN HUMANITIES PRESS

Open Humanities Press is an international, scholar-led open access publishing collective whose mission is to make leading works of contemporary critical thought freely available worldwide.
More at http://openhumanitiespress.org/

Contents

Acknowledgements 7

List of Figures 9

Mediation, Mutation and Decomposition:
  An Introduction 11

1. Performing Fungi Media 43

2. Fungoid Decomposition as a
   Form of Post-Internet Biomediation 71

3. The Dungeons of Polymorphous Pan 121

4. Fungosexual Replication Beyond the Internet 188

Conclusion 247

Works Cited 259

Acknowledgements

The vital life for my research into fungi media was provided by the London squatting movement, which created cultural and material conditions for my philosophical-performative pursuit over the last decade. I am hugely indebted to it. More specifically, I would like to thank a couple of hundred performers who engaged with the sewage space of the Dungeons of Polymorphous Pan, and a couple of thousand participants in the Chronic Illness events who were involved in the shared corporeality with fungoids down there. I hope that the micropolitical posthuman entities that unfolded at our squat can spread their infectious potential to other spaces.

Moreover, I am grateful to Joanna Zylinska, who has been discussing my cryptic ideas all along and who has directly influenced the development of this text. If this book says something close to clear, it is probably thanks to her.

List of Figures

Fig. 1. Piotr Bockowski, 2019. Mouldy print from *3Decay* at Chronic Illness 12.

Fig. 2. Piotr Bockowski, 2019. Photograph from a video from *Holobiont* projected on a rotten pile at the Dungeons of Polymorphous Pan, Chronic Illness 11: Hollow Soils.

Fig. 3. Magda Durka, 2016. Collage of photos of *Synthetic Organs* (2016); performance by Piotr Bockowski at the Chronic Illness of Mysterious Origin 4.

Fig. 4. E. H. Dixon, 1837. *The Great Dust Heap* at Wellcome Collection (Public Domain).

Fig. 5. Mike Pelletier, 2016. Still from *Performance Capture 2*.

Fig. 6. Robert Hooke, 1665. Scan of the original print of microfungus Mucor; hand drawing from *Micrographia* based on observations via handmade microscope (Public Domain).

Fig. 7. Yasmine Akim, 2018. *Ooze Feed* directed by Piotr Bockowski and Alex Avery.

Fig. 8. Piotr Bockowski, 2017. Fungoid life at the Dungeons of Polymorphous Pan.

Fig. 9. Piotr Bockowski, 2016. Promotional image for the Chronic Illness of Mysterious Origin 4 event, featuring documentation of *Holobiont*.

Fig. 10. HTV, 2017. Photography of the *Synthetic Organs* act by Piotr Bockowski.

Fig. 11. The Institution of Rot (Richard Crow), 1994. Visual presentation of the space of the Institution of Rot in *TimeOut London* in 1994.

Figs 12–22. Piotr Bockowski, 2019. *3Decay* series, with technical assistance from NeonM3.

Fig. 23. Piotr Bockowski, 2019. Fungal media symerging life forms at the Dungeons of Polymorphous Pan.

Fig. 24. Officina Corpuscoli, 2019. *Continuous Bodies – Bodies of Change – mycelium shroud with fungal growth* ©Officina_Corpuscoli_Maurizio_Montalti.

Fig. 25. Bonnie Bakeneko, 2019. Online auto-cannibalism of female nipples.

Fig. 26. Loi Wang, 2017. *Holobiont* video projection on the body of Piotr Bockowski.

INTRODUCTION

Mediation, Mutation and Decomposition

This book examines how our understanding of human sexuality and human body changes through the processes of mediation unfolding at the intersection of nonhuman life and the Internet. It analyses performances and simulations of human subjectivity, as well as digital image manipulation strategies that generate novel visions of bodily and sexual mutations, in the context of new materialist philosophies – especially those focusing on dark materialities and posthumanism. Such philosophies employ the concept of the material dynamics of nonhuman life as a speculative tool to engage with technological mediations. There is a radical nonhuman dimension to the performances of bodily mutations on the part of some Internet users. I am interested in examining those mutations as a way of probing various new possibilities of life, in its corporeal and sexual dimensions. With a view to this, I turn to fungi as a conceptual device which offers some crucial insights into the generativity of living matter. Fungi play a fundamental role in the decomposition of ecologies. They can process the most complex organic bodily forms, including potentially toxic or polluting bio-compounds, break them down and enable new mutant fusions. In this way, fungi revitalise environments by getting rid of obsolete body structures, releasing bioenergy into circulation and making this energy available for other life forms. My work aims to translate those fungal behaviours into visual and conceptual strategies for rethinking human subjectivity, in particular human sexuality and the human body, on and off the Internet. The concept of 'fungi media' will serve for me as a figuration for articulating those transformative processes.

'Fungi media' is thus offered in this book as a framing device for my theory of the technological decomposition of human sexuality and the human body, and for my analysis of their mediations on the Internet. Those mediations, actualised by performances of bodily mutations, serve for me as performative speculations about the nonsexual forms of human reproduction. In my work, which involves conceptual speculation enacted with words as well as artistic acts by myself and others, I am interested in investigating those aspects of contemporary visual media culture that explore the idea of nonsexual transhuman reproduction through the processes of bodily disintegration, fragmentation and multiplication. I perceive those 'mutant performances' as being supported by the manipulation techniques of social communication and the extreme bodily imagery available on the Internet. What I see as the 'mutagenic influence of the Internet' is not just related to the *visual* shapeshifting of Internet users' bodies; it also concerns the integrity of human sexual identities – which become fractured, dispersed, multiplied and fluidly hybrid.

My book is thus concerned with the simultaneous challenge posed to human sexual identities by networked communication *and* by the mutations of human bodily imagery online and offline. Those two phenomena of human technological activity – the dispersion of sexualities by means of networked communication *and* the image manipulation of mutant bodies by means of computer simulation and editing – are related to fungal decomposition not merely via aesthetic correspondence but also, more importantly, through their shared mobilisation of new materialist thinking about the human body. This thinking can take Internet users beyond the Internet and towards some novel forms of involvement with nonhuman life. Commenting on how physical art can convey the mediation of human bodies online, such as the circulation of images with accompanying various distortions, transfers and interactions, post-Internet artist Martijn Hendriks argues that 'these issues translate themselves into questions of disintegration and contamination' (Hendriks and Novitskova 2014) in a direct material sense. My work thus aims to capture the transgression of contemporary philosophy and performance art beyond Internet culture – and towards a nonhuman, fungal life. Human sexuality and the human body serve as terrains on which this transgression will be studied throughout this book.

Fungal Figuration

My concept of 'fungi media' can be understood as a conceptual 'figuration' of posthuman subjectivity, in the sense of the term proposed by Rosi Braidotti. Her notion of 'figuration' (Braidotti 2019) describes the becoming of posthuman subjects who are not defined by universalist or normative models of subjectivity (which are considered to be shaped by 'humanist' assumptions by her), but rather by the 'nomadic processes' of monistic vitalism (Braidotti 2019, 43). The 'fungi media' figuration aims to theorise such subjectivities. Specifically, I look at the technological mediations of the human body on the Internet, in conjunction with the body's mediations by the microbial organisation of bio-life. In other words, the theoretical and material conjunction of the entanglement of networked media and microbes in transforming human subjectivities is the specific focus of my work. I call this entanglement 'fungal' because, as explained above, fungi are of vital importance to the life unfolding on our planet. They expose the primal life processes occurring on a microbial scale and present those processes to humans for macroscale perception – the way media technologies do in more than one way.

Braidotti's concept of posthuman subjectivity is based on the monistic and vitalist ontology of radical 'material immanence' (Braidotti 2019, 34). Her subjectivity is considered 'naturecultural', referring as it does to the deep rootedness of all human activity in biological activity as well as to the inherent intelligence of all vital material processes. By conceptualising media technologies as extensions of microbial bodies and by theorising microbes as inherently intelligent, I corroborate Braidotti's proposition that cultural phenomena are biologically embodied and that all living matter manifests intelligence (Braidotti 2019, 43). In this materialistic and vitalist understanding, subjectivity becomes posthuman as it is not only defined by relations between humans. Instead, it also involves nonhumans, such as technology, animals, plants and other biological entities on our planet: fungi and microbes. This process of transhuman becoming with other forms of living matter involves a conceptual 'de-familiarisation' (46) of subjects. Braidotti calls this framework 'zoe-geo-centered' (42), where 'geo' stands for Earth and 'zoe' – for the bodies living on it. This framework defines posthuman subjectivity as a dynamic process in the sense of geographical movement (which she calls 'nomadism') as well as in the sense of the transmutation of living bodies, which enter into a variety of assemblages with each other and with their socio-technological context. Braidotti's figuration offers a dramatisation of becoming with regard to a pluralist posthuman subjectivity. Reflecting on the performance of that becoming, my figuration of 'fungi media' focuses on the nonsexual reproduction of human bodies by means of media mutation. As part of my process, I offer a conceptual cross-pollination of the theories of microbes and media studies, using concepts borrowed from microbiology but applied, precisely *as concepts*, to media theory. This transdisciplinary experiment supports my theoretical effort to position human subjectivity as a transhuman hybrid in the process of becoming with microbes and technology.

Post-Internet

Involving microbial evolutions in media theory, my research into fungi media develops the proposition that human technological civilisation has to acknowledge and perform a better understanding of life processes in order to survive. To approach this problem, my work proposes, as part of its method, an artistic performance in which the subjectivities of human performers are redefined by entering into degrees of intimacy with nonhuman life entities. This method employs theatrical enactments of bodily mutation within a performance space, which is itself conceptualised as a living entity. This conceptual approach allows for the movements of the performers' bodies to be perceived as animated by, and as becoming part of, a nonhuman life that exceeds the limits of human bodies. Importantly, my experiments with performance art are influenced by the aesthetics of bodily mutation. This aesthetics is derived from the severely manipulated digital images of human bodies proliferating on the Internet. This is why I consider those acts as a form of post-Internet practice: they borrow an Internet visuality and aesthetics, which is then applied to real-life practices. This corporeal reenactment of online bodily mutations calls for the examination of the human involvement with Internet-related technological infrastructures beyond the frameworks of screen simulation – and towards a more tangible and comprehensive engagement with life processes.

The term 'post-Internet' was introduced by writer James Bridle in their blog 'New Aesthetics' in May 2011 (Bridle 2011). Since then it has been discussed globally throughout the second decade of the 21st century, especially in the art circles. The manifesto of the comprehensive 'Art Post-Internet' exhibition, organised at the UCCA in Beijing in collaboration with Goethe Institute China in 2014, summarises the concept by noticing that 'post-internet refers not to a time "after the internet" but rather to the internet state of mind – to think in the fashion of the network' (Archey and Peckham 2014). Post-Internet art reflects on various processes and phenomena related to the Internet, but it embodies them in material practices, seeking new understandings of materiality via thinking about the Internet. Applying this term to performance art, I use the concept of 'post-Internet' performance as a strategy involving the remediation of the human body – towards the digital body of the posthuman. In my understanding, post-Internet bodily performance can reclaim the supposedly 'de-materialised' body of humans who are being mediated by increasingly complex databases and other forms of digital media that are seemingly detached from physiology. Post-Internet performance thus offers an opportunity to re-materialise the bodies of Internet users, at the same time as harvesting the experience of Internet mediations. The concept also provides an important opportunity to reflect on Internet infrastructures and experiences in relation to the crucial materialities of life. Answering the question: 'What does materiality mean in the post-internet era?', Martijn Hendriks notices that there is a very particular 'kind of materiality that is produced by processes aiming for dematerialisation' (Hendriks and Novitskova 2014). This kind of materiality reveals a strangeness of material objects, which in turn conveys complex subjectivities of non-individual but potentially living entities. In other words, abstract processes of the Internet can also materialise as distributed processes of life. Artist Katja Novitskova adds that, as we realise that the 'digital image consumes fossil fuels' (Hendriks and Novitskova 2014), screen simulations also need to be seen as physiological. Bearing this realisation in mind, my engagement with fungi media is an attempt to provide an account of the remediation of human sexuality and the human body by nonhuman life.

Conceptually and politically, my work is driven by an anti-modernist approach to technology. It explores the possibility of reevaluating technological mediations of the human body by directing attention towards nonhuman life as the very basis of the constitution of human technology and human bodies alike. My inquiry is positioned against the uncritical idea of progress or acceleration, proposing instead to explore the narratives of decomposition unfolding across various levels of the biosphere and the processes of the techno-devolution of humans that are entangled with them. I see the importance of offering such a philosophical position which foregrounds media decomposition in being able to challenge the industrialist belief in progress, with a view to imagining some more viable strategies of multispecies living in technologically mediated environments. By doing so, I want to promote aesthetic decadence as an approach to life, an approach that also proposes a withdrawal from sexual reproduction.

The performances of media mutations which constitute the subject of my study and the practice part of the project aim to challenge the cultural narratives based on the productivist and consumerist values of fertile families. One of the main theoretical premises of my work is the recognition of the bodily manipulation unfolding on the Internet, understood in terms of a reproduction that is not sexual. This idea of bodily mutation via the Internet is developed from Marshall McLuhan's understanding of media as bodily processes. In its pursuit of materialist vitalism, my narrative about fungi media locates human sexuality in the wider generative potentiality of nonhuman life. My overall project is inspired by the conviction that, by recognising the nonhuman nature of thinking and technology, we humans can develop a better quality of life on our planet – one that will be better both for us *and* the planet. Embracing mutant performance as an alternative form of human bodily reproduction can arguably lead not only to decreasing the size of the human population but also to the lowering of the environmental impact of our civilisation, which could possibly turn us away from the consumerist-productivist depletion of the natural resources, and towards an aesthetic appreciation of the decomposition processes of life. My art practice is also intended to explore the possibility of the performative reworking of the issues related to the threat of human extinction through the media-cultural phenomena of mutant bodily performance.

Fungosexuality

By focusing on the aesthetics of corporeal mutation and decomposition in digital image manipulations on the Internet (traced from their origin in bodily performance and bioart), I want to reflect on the sexualisation of diverse bodily transformations that occur through online activity. Looking at the proliferation of Internet pornography, with its accelerating fetishisms, a rapidly growing number of new non-binary gender identities, the convergence of queer sexualities with technophile subcultures, the fantasies of cybersex and alien abduction, I conceptualise the Internet as a sphere of the transgression of human sexuality. I also propose that humans subjected to, or taking on, Internet mediations can be considered as 'beyond-sexual' life entities, which in turn leads me to suggest that the medium of the Internet offers a mode of human bodily reproduction that is not sexual. To account for the online transgressions of sexuality I introduce the concept of 'fungosexuality'. This notion becomes a conceptual device, or another figuration of sorts, that will help me interpret the mutant aesthetics of Internet bodies while opening up onto a more extensive planetary account of the material grounding of different technologies (including the Internet) and their relation to the biosphere. The aim of my work is thus to accentuate the bio-materiality of technological mediations and their multifaceted transhuman corporeality, with a view to outlining a model for a better way of living with technomedia, one that resists what Braidotti has called 'the commodification of life' and its deadly 'overcoding by capitalist profit principle' (Braidotti 2019, 42).

Specifically, I ask whether post-Internet performances of bodily mutation can be considered a form of bodily reproduction – offered here as a counterpoint to the 'capitalist' overproduction of sexual bodies which causes global overpopulation and, ultimately, has a destructive impact on nonhuman life. 'Fungosexuality' serves as a name for this possibility of bodily reproduction via mutant performance. Witnessing the proliferation of non-binary sexualities, fetishism, gender-queering and asexuality on the social media platforms of the Internet, I am interested in how this proliferation converges around visions of the mutation of the human body. The transgression of the binary understanding of sexuality on the Internet unfolds in parallel with the complex challenges that human subjectivities face online and offline. The interfaces of social media platforms offer multifaceted techniques for the reconfiguration of users' fragmented subjectivities in the form of their multiple 'profiles'. Via social media, the Internet becomes a theatre – and a fitting illustration of what Judith Butler has described as a 'performative construction' of gender *and* sex (Butler 1990). Butler initially distinguishes biological sex from a socially constructed gender, which is a script of sexual preferences, sensitivities and expressions. She then suggests that biological sex cannot exist without its actualisation in gender performance. Taking that into account, social media offer a perfect opportunity for performing such a construction of gender, allowing for modifications of sexual expressions that are detached from the determinism of biological sex but that remain contextualised and controlled by the technology of Internet platforms. Nevertheless, in my view elaborate gender constructs created by means of social media become increasingly disconnected from the idea of biological sex. Internet environments invite sophisticated, hybrid and ambiguous constructs of sexual desire and fetishism that exist within computer databases but that remain separated from the physiologies of Internet users' bodies.

With regard to this latter point, the vital aim of my work is to foreground the very material aspect of the asexuality of Internet users – those who decide to perform mutant aesthetics online and those who do so in physical spaces. I want to examine those mutant bodily forms that are being born at the crossroads of Internet culture and bodily performance art as lending themselves to a philosophical speculation about the abstraction of human bodily reproduction, which is achieved through the transgression of biological sex, but also through a new materiality of the performing bodies. This new materiality is manifested by the intimacy between mutant performers and nonhuman, fungoid life forms. In my study, I take into consideration diverse expressions of gender-bending online, which are enacted with a view to then translating them into bodily performance *beyond the Internet*. In my own practice of performing a mutant body, I situate the hybrid and fractured subjectivities characteristic of the Internet in the context of material vitalism. Indeed, I want to research those subjectivities not as human social constructs but rather as performative expressions of the primal generativity of matter. Employing the philosophies of dark materialism, I aim to theorise the Internet and the human bodies entangled with it in the context of the material processes of nonhuman life. Finally, my concept of fungosexuality encapsulates the possibility of making connections between post-Internet queer mutants and the extreme diversity of the pre-sexual forms of bodily reproduction performed by fungi.

My thesis is that performing the above-mentioned bodily mutations on and through the Internet taps into primal (by which I specifically mean *fungal*) vitality via the multiplication of fractured and hybrid subjectivities online first, but also through the explicit reshaping of performers' bodies. The latter involves erasing the features of their human (binary) sexuality and adding computer-simulated nonhuman features. The fracturing and hybridisation of bodies is inherent to networked communication unfolding on the Internet. The proliferation of such images and tropes introduces a form of reproduction of mediated human bodies which is not sexual. Human bodies online are exposed to the hollowing of human subjectivity through their opening to a mergence with nonhuman entities. I propose that this mergence of human bodies with diverse living entities afforded by the Internet offers a novel form of sexualised expression, which I call 'fungal'. In my work I'm thus focusing on those forms of bodily performance which are inspired by such hybrid Internet visuality, and which manipulate the image and concept of the human body to present it as partly nonhuman. Many performers addressing nonhuman life identify as sexually 'queer' or 'non-binary'. They embrace their nonhuman identity as 'mutants' on social media, where they digitally reproduce their mutant bodies by nonsexual (in a binary, reproductive sense) means.

In our biosphere, the material process of decomposition is driven by fungi. This process is of key importance to the creation of new life forms. This is why decomposition becomes crucial for me as a concept, visual image and, last but not least, a set of material processes in my own performance practice. The latter is aimed at enacting human sexuality and the human body differently, by breaking them down and reshaping them in a new form. Yet this process is not just mine. The mutant performances of many other Internet users are sustained by the media decomposition of their human bodies and identities, with their body images transformed into weird shapes. The decomposing (i.e., fungal) element of technological mediations manifests itself in various performances of bodily mutations, offering the possibility of the non-sexual reproduction of those bodies via their multiple mutant shapes. Those mutant performances can be perceived as sexualised in a queer way, but at the same time they involve an intense fetishisation of the mutant features of the performers. I introduce the term 'fungosexuality', instead of using non- or a-sexuality, to highlight this very transformation of human sexuality towards various 'beyond-sexual' forms of bodily reproduction associated with fungal entities. In other words, I understand fungosexuality as offering a shift from humans' sexual mode of bodily reproduction and towards post-sexual mutations by means of media performance. Since sexualised practices of fetishism, queer sex and trans challenge the traditional reproduction of human bodies via the coupling of binary genitals, they arguably can be more prone to reinvesting their actors' reproductive creativity in the media performance of some alternative ways of being together. I conceptualise this phenomenon in terms of a resistance against the productivist and consumerist use of technology, in particular by opposing my concept of the fungosexual transgression of human identities to the sexual overproduction of humans on our planet today.

Vitality and Dark Materialism

I ground my theorisation of fungi media in various accounts of the vitality of matter and distributed intelligence within material processes of life, with a view to contextualising the understanding of techno-media environments and exposing their generative potency. My media-theoretical background comes from theories of media technologies understood as extensions and modifications of bodily processes (McLuhan 2001), of media positioned as environmental infrastructures and circulations of material elements (Peters 2015), and of media seen as life-generating environments (Mitchell 2010). All these theories assist me in conceptually embedding media technologies in the landscape of discussion around vitalist materialism.

With all this, the aim of my investigation into fungi media is to contribute to the 21st century academic and artistic discussion around nonhuman life and its growing theoretical significance in defining human subjectivity. In other words, my work looks at a variety of concepts at the cross-section between new media technologies and philosophies of dark materialism, in an attempt to examine possible connections between media and processes of biological life. This will in turn help me explain the phenomenon of post-Internet mutant performance, which is framed both by Internet practices and the agency of nonhuman life. To clarify, 'dark' materialisms (Alaimo 2010, Artaud 1995, Barad 2007, Bellmer 2005, Haraway 2016, Land 2011, Latour 1999, Morton 2017, Negarestani 2008, Thacker 2010, Tsing 2015, Woodard 2012a) interrogate material processes defining human life through placing philosophical emphasis on the agency of living bodies that are other than human, and through recognising those bodies as acting beyond the control of, or even the ability to be exhaustively explained by, rational human subjectivity. My aim in engaging with dark materialist philosophies is to account for the deep imbrications of human technologies within the fabric of life on our planet. I aim to achieve this by engaging with media theories that shift the conceptualisation of media beyond their traditional understanding as communication devices – and towards their role as mediators of the generative vitality of nonhuman bodies.

The understanding of media technologies in relation to life has been discussed since the introduction of Marshall McLuhan's idea that media were extensions of human bodies about half a century ago. Around the same time, biologist Lynn Margulis started developing her revolutionary theory of symbiotic evolution (Margulis 2001), explaining how human bodies, as well as all other living macro-bodies, were co-dependent with the dynamic and diverse networks of microbial entities. Now, as much as I'm bouncing off McLuhan's postulated closeness of media to human bodies, my principal aim is to stress the microbial understanding of the processes of mediation. With this, I propose a philosophical interpretation of human technologies through the microbial context of communication networks – and through offering an understanding of media as processes of life.

McLuhan proposed that human media technologies were extending, infiltrating and modifying human bodies. In this perspective all communication methods, symbolic systems and civilisational advancements are presented as life processes that are involved in changing human bodies, processes which McLuhan called 'extensions' of bodies. McLuhan's concept of mediatic extensions describes an ecological relation defined by the progression of time, where 'new' media extend 'old' ones as their environments. New media thus create environments that condition and modify old media, according to McLuhan, including the oldest medium – that of the human body. My narrative about fungi media thus starts with questioning the integrity of the human body and with exposing microbial processes as vital to understanding humans and their media technologies.

Microbes are important in this analysis not only because they precede humans evolutionarily but also because they continuously play a crucial role in making and supporting the life functions of human bodies. Taking this fact into account, human bodies can be described as extensions of microbial entities. Moreover, in a wider perspective, human media technologies can also be understood as extensions of microbial entities. I am thus offering here a particular interpretation of McLuhan's ideas, one that connects to Margulis' theory of the evolution of microbial life. With this, I focus on aspects of communication, intelligence and creativity which are inherent to the primal forms of life and which are manifested again in new technological forms of human media, represented for me here by the Internet. A significant aspect of my work involves posing a challenge to the belief in an autonomous human subjectivity and a unified sense of the human's bodily integrity in order to expose the microbial entities that are constantly at work in supporting what we know as human life and the human body.

Human technologies interfere in processes of non-human life. They originate from human ideas about life and change countless multitudes of life forms at the same time. Questions of discovery (via techniques of scientific experimentation and technological inventions) with regard to different aspects of life are closely intertwined with concerns about redefining life. In my work I'm greatly inspired by theories of fungi ecologies, as analysed by mycologist Paul Stamets in his book, *Mycelium Running* (Stamets 2005). I am not evaluating the scientific accuracy of his argument here but rather translating his observations about fungi into a theoretical vehicle of my own. I follow Stamets' choice of fungi to theoretically represent the whole of microbial life, as fungi mediate microscale life for humans by presenting it for our macroscale experience. They are also the major decomposer amongst organisms on our planet. My reading of Stamets, through McLuhan and Margulis, aims to interrogate *not so much how human the media are* (as extensions of the human body), but rather *how nonhumanly fungoid the media can be* (as framed by processes of decomposition).

Stamets' excitement about the possibilities of improving various living environments, some of which involve significantly increasing the quality of human life, is instrumental for my attempt to ground my philosophical perspective in media such as the Internet, with a view to offering a sustainable understanding of human technology and a sustainable approach to the biosphere. According to Stamets' concept of ecology, the production and consumption of bodies within the biosphere, globally as well as within particular environments, is possible primarily thanks to complementary processes of decomposition. The processes of decomposition are ground processes performed by fungal and microbial entities. They undo complex life forms and disperse the fragmented bio-particles within the evolutionary cycles of transmutation. Recognising the overwhelming civilisational issues of industrially accelerated overproduction of things and bodies (e.g., in human and nonhuman farming), which are stimulated by the cultural politics of mass consumption and by so-called 'family values', I seek to understand technological infrastructures and, in particular, media communications, in the context of decomposition processes described by Stamets. Drawing on the understanding of decomposition as coming from fungal ecologies, I experiment with technologically-mediated mutant bodily performance, with a view to developing a new theory-practice method for my work.

Bodily Performance as a Philosophy of the Nonhuman

Alongside my theoretical argument, my art practice offers a non-linguistic form of engagement with the concept of nonhuman intelligence unfolding behind media processes. In this book I reflect upon my own bodily performance by examining it as a sequence of human-nonhuman acts converging with microbial activity. Here, the practice part of my work is strongly inspired by the idea of the visceral decomposition of human thought pursued by Antonin Artaud (Barber 2013). Artaud understood all theoretical reflection as a gestural figuration of the nonhuman processes mediated by the human body. He saw the nature of those processes, such as the plague or his guts, as quintessentially microbial. Similarly, Eugene Thacker confronts in his writing 'the world without humans' (Thacker 2010), although conveyed within human bodies by nonhuman microorganisms: 'bacteria, fungi, and a whole bestiary of other organisms' (Thacker 2010, 7). Thacker then effectively proposes 'that thought is not human' (7). This suggestion provocatively reminds us that brain processes, just like many other crucial processes of the human body, including digestion and the immune system's performance, are determined by microbial entities living within humans. Moreover, Thacker speculates that intelligence can have pre-human, beyond-human or even posthuman material forms. Philosophy, the radical expression of human intelligence, meets here its linguistic limitations as it cannot express certain dimensions of life within its own language, according to Thacker. This diagnosed limitation is also his reason for using figures of poetic description borrowed from science fiction or horror novels in his philosophical writings about nonhuman life. In this way, Thacker offers horror writing as a non-philosophical form of philosophy about nonhuman life. Elaborating on the proclaimed horror of philosophy, evoked by human attempts to think of themselves as transgressing towards the nonhuman, Thacker points out a certain advantage of mediation which is enacted not through abstract concepts but through 'impossible life forms – mist, ooze, blobs, slime, clouds, and muck' (Thacker 2010, 9) – or, as Ben Woodard puts it, 'fungoids' (Woodard 2012a). Those entities convey certain forms of intelligent performance, which I use as a conceptual tool to map human mediations on the Internet.

My aim with this is not to postulate a fixed ontological relationship between the Internet and fungi but rather to find a more tangible approach to human technologies of communication, one that accounts for the latter's environmental impact. This is why I include in my theory a number of philosophical figurations and speculations around issues concerning the entanglement of the Internet within the key processes of life performed by fungoids. Iranian philosopher Reza Negarestani goes so far as to propose, in his speculative fiction *Cyclonopedia* (Negarestani 2008), that the whole of human civilisation, with its advanced technological infrastructures and abstract media communications, is secretly animated by a mysterious substance of living blobs, pressed into deep layers of the geological biosphere. His work, alongside Artaud's theory of performance and some other dark-materialist philosophies of nonhuman vitalism, have led me to see technological mediations of human bodies on the Internet, such as networked communication and the transformation of human subjectivity, as processes that remain intertwined with nonhuman bodies – and that simultaneously mediate nonhuman forms of intelligence.

The practice part of my work develops a performative method of bodily movement, space curation and creative writing that is inspired by Internet phenomena, which are positioned in this book as body-media mutations. As mentioned above, those online mutations involve a visual decomposition and a reinvention of Internet users' bodies, processes which are being afforded by the growing accessibility of various editing tools, interaction platforms, exploratory environments and digital scanners. In my artistic practice I re-embody those mutations through my own physiological bodily performances within a bioactive performance space, conceptualising in this way the scattered processes of fungoid life. This re-embodiment of Internet aesthetics in real-life performances – performances which are then recorded and posted to the Internet in the form of videos – inscribes them in the 'post-Internet' framework, which I outlined earlier.

I had been involved in bodily performance for many years and had also been active in the squatting movement, but my practice and my living situation took a unique turn at the time of commencing this work. While initiating this research project on fungi media in 2015, I squatted a rotten sewage space, in which I have been dwelling together with a variety of microbial life forms such as slimes and fungi since then. I've also been organising performance and biomedia events there, inviting humans online to immerse themselves in the living network of urban decay, or partake in 'alien abduction acts'. Performers and participants in the Chronic Illness (Chronic Illness 2023) events, as I have called them, have been drawn from the media networks such as Facebook, through which I have encouraged users to move beyond the screens of their computers and meet at my space (called 'The Dungeons of Polymorphous Pan' on social media). By encouraging this move, I don't intend to manifest any naive abandonment of technology with the intention of returning to some utopian pre-Internet past-time of human communality. On the contrary, what interests me in my practice is the mediated, post-Internet reworking of human subjectivity with and through media technologies.

Performers and participants in the Chronic Illness events come together within my fungi-populated space. Here, a new life process that is decidedly less human and much more affiliated with microbial entities takes place. The performers and the participants open up to an encounter with the mysterious nonhumans within them and the environment, which is mediated by and with technology. Through this, we could go so far as to suggest that they are no-longer-human, at least temporarily. I perceive these acts as being part of speculative forms of research into nonhuman life, which is being conducted through an embodied practice as much as through concepts and written texts.

A Summary of Chapters

This book is divided into four chapters. Chapter 1 explains *my performative approach to media*, using my bodily performance. It outlines my perspective on the technologies of communication by presenting them not as mere artefacts (i.e., human tools) but rather as performances of subtle life processes, as inspired by the book *Life After New Media* by Sarah Kember and Joanna Zylinska (2012). Each of the following three chapters of the book has a conceptual lead that explores a specific theoretical dimension of the problem of bodily mutation in performance. Chapter 2 focuses on *fungal decomposition* as the key concept and process underpinning mediation. Chapter 3 explains the theme of *the Chronic Illness*, which is the title of the bodily performance events I have curated and participated in. Chapter 4 brings to the fore my concept of *fungosexuality*.

A narrative about the possibility of theorising media in the context of the philosophies of microbial life and, particularly, the body of fungi, is developed in Chapter 2. This is where I experiment with speculative philosophical reflection, applied to probe the extent to which it is possible to trace an analogy between the influence of the Internet and other media technologies on the humans on the one hand and the networked 'running' of mycelium within the biosphere on the other. I approach communication technologies through an exploration of processes such as the network behaviour of mycelium, the ubiquity of microbiota in the biosphere, the role of fungal rot in ecosystems, interspecies relations amongst microbes, symbiotic evolutions, non-sexual forms of reproduction, immediate mutations, and, last but not least, life organised in the form of trans-individual entities. Exploring parallels between media and fungal ecologies, I open the question of the deep involvement of human communication technologies with the primal forms of life. This involvement enfolds the generative potency of media environments and opens them up to a vitalist understanding. It also prepares the philosophical ground for framing humans' involvement with the Internet as a process of bodily reproduction by means other than binary sex. Eventually, it leads me to position post-Internet bodily aesthetics in performance art as an enactment of non-binary sexualities, one that fetishises nonhuman bodily features and the overall decomposition of the human body. This mutant fetishism is explained as offering a deeply ecological reflection on human and nonhuman life forms.

As a meeting point of nonhuman life and human communication technologies, my own performance and bodily media practice is investigated in Chapter 3. The investigation revolves around the conceptualisation of the bioactive performance art space in the Dungeons of Polymorphous Pan, offering a critical reading of the practice unfolding in this space. Drawing on several human bodily acts, I situate them in the context of minute life activity in order to find out what can be said about the condition of human existence through focusing on microbial and fungal life entities – and on the human impact on nonhumans. Specifically, the microbial life activity is considered to be the key performance unfolding in the space, where the human acts, some of them highly sexualised, serve as an environmental context for it. Analysing my own body act *Synthetic Organs* and the bioart installation *Holobiont* in this chapter, I position those acts as performances of microbes themselves. The general aim of this chapter is to examine and explain why it is worth focusing on performing human subjectivity (including human sexuality and the body) with microbial bodies in academic and artistic research on media technologies.

The initial question of the embodiment of fungoid bodies in media technologies will lead me in the final part of this book to a consideration of those media as a form of 'fungosexual' reproduction. Chapter 4 plays with the idea of the Internet enacting the advent of biotechnologies that revive microbial forms of reproduction, such as nonsexual cloning or other forms of beyond-sexual replication. The final chapter searches for answers to the question of replication by means of technologically-facilitated androgynous mutations of sex, mutations which transgress culturally-structured notions of sexuality. My exploration of fetishist sexuality in various media focuses on what cloning means in the context of the Internet. Is there such a thing as human sexuality without reproduction as its foundational feature – and is there human reproduction without sex? I interrogate the characteristics of accelerated mutability on the Internet, touching on phenomena such as the proliferation of digital avatars, queer media, cybersex, genetic engineering and the fragmentation of identities online. Paying particular attention to how trans fetishism in the media pictures the decomposition of cultural frameworks by means of technologies such as the Internet, I reference a number of artistic bodily transmutations developed online. This leads me to a discussion of selected examples of bodily performance and bioart as strategies for developing new philosophies of technology.

The Art Practice of Fungi Media

The three selected examples from my wider artistic practice have been chosen with a view to demonstrating in a most rounded way my attempt to enact the key concepts discussed in this book. Importantly, they all focus on my own work as a body performer. They also all foreground the activities unfolding within the performance space of the Dungeons of Polymorphous Pan. The fungi-inhabited space of the Dungeons itself becomes an active participant in the performances – and thus also in my overall work.

1. *3Decay* is an experiment in creating what I call 'fungi media art'. It was conducted at the Dungeons of Polymorphous Pan, a sewage space in North London, which I squatted in 2015 and which I have been curating as a venue for

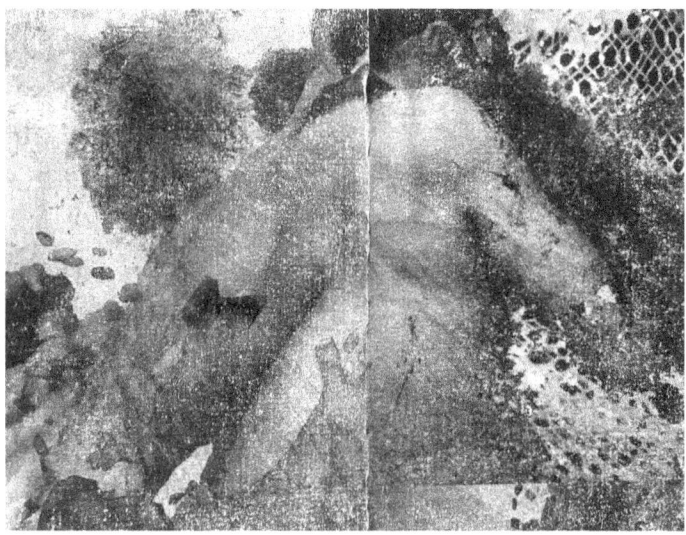

Fig. 1. Piotr Bockowski, 2019.
Mouldy print from *3Decay* at Chronic Illness 12.

mutant performance. The space has also served as a thought laboratory for my speculative philosophy about nonhuman life entities. For the purposes of this book, I have documented and reflected upon the fungi-infested abandoned architecture of the Dungeons, mediating the entanglement of human civilisation with the life forms that host it. The documentation takes the form of 3D scans of my body, which have been computer-edited, using photographs of fungoid bodies taken within the space and some digital distortions simulating the microbes. The scans have been inserted as separate pages between chapters 3 and 4.

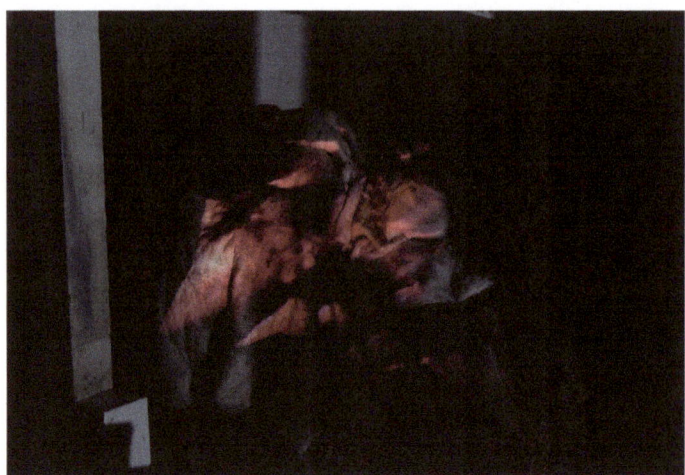

Fig. 2. Piotr Bockowski, 2019. Photograph of *a* video from *Holobiont* projected on a rotten pile at the Dungeons of Polymorphous Pan, Chronic Illness II: Hollow Soils.

2   *Holobiont* is a biomedia art installation developed in the Dungeons of Polymorphous Pan. It transforms piles of rotten material that has accumulated in the space during the time of its occupation into heaps of living blob matter. The material hosts a diversity of microbial life forms and is fed by various body traces of human participants and performers who enter the space. The video of humanoid body parts is reflected on the surface of biological debris, animating the rot visually. The *Holobiont* video is a compilation of excerpts from a number of bioart installations that took place at the Dungeons of Polymorphous Pan between 2016-2019.

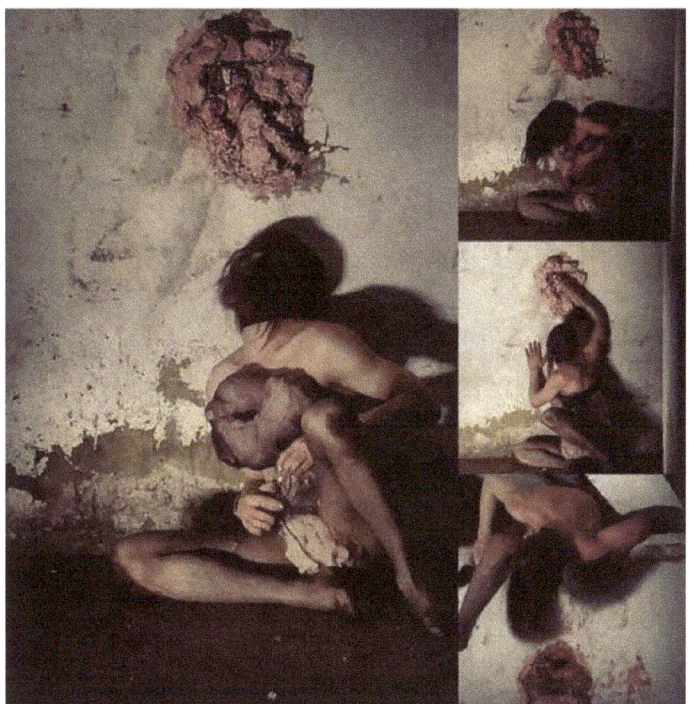

Fig. 3. Magda Durka, 2016. Collage of photos of *Synthetic Organs* (2016) performance by Piotr Bockowski at Chronic Illness of Mysterious Origin 4.

3 *Synthethic Organs* is a body act that originated in the Dungeons of Polymorphous Pan. The naked body of the performer is extended with loosely attached amorphous 'organs', made out of fungi-infested synthetic materials. During the act the organs are moving around the performer's body, provoking a variety of movements, reactions and expressions. Those movements define the performer's body in terms of its relationship to the fungoid environment of

the performance space. The organs had been sourced from a large wound sculpted into the wall of the Dungeons. They mediate the space as a living entity that hosts the body of the performer, which has been fragmented by the mutability of synthetic organs.

CHAPTER I

Performing Fungi Media

Sexualities of Mutants

My research into fungi media poses a question about the extent to which the mediation of human bodies on and by the Internet is embedded in, and embodies, basic life forms. I propose that human bodies can be described as fungi media, as, on the one hand, they are being shaped and connected by the Internet while, on the other, they remain linked with and by fungi and other microbes (aka 'the mycelium Internet'). As mentioned in the Introduction, the term 'fungi media' serves as a figuration that describes the re-materialisation of the Internet through the performative involvement of human bodies with fungal entities. I study this relation with a particular focus on the field of performance art.

My approach is based on the application of the concept of 'post-Internet art' to my own and other performers' mutant bodily practice, which I deploy in my work to enact what I describe as 'fungosexuality'. Fungosexuality, as outlined earlier, is a term I propose to refer to forms of bodily performance art that fetishise a transhuman presentation of the performers' bodies, meshing bodily mutation with rot. Fungosexuality embraces the aesthetics of androgyny and other forms of sexual ambiguity. I consider it a form of queer sexuality, as it disconnects sexualisation of the body from the reproductive features of binary human sex, linking it instead with transhuman reproduction through performative mutations and decomposition.

I build my concept of fungosexuality from the selected references to contemporary materialist philosophies, media and cultural critique as well as bioscience concepts that have had a key influence on posthumanist thinking in the humanities. I draw on texts that, in my view, have made an important contribution to shaping the posthuman imaginary.

The mutant performance, which I involve in my art practice, references the technological manipulation of human bodies and their interspecies entanglement. It incorporates a variety of imaginary creaturely features and a more abstract bio-morphology into artistic bodily forms. The themes of interspecies entanglement reflect on the symbiotic relations of fungi with humans and other organisms. The hybrid coexistence of fungi with other species, which I explore in my work, serves as the basis for environmental generativity. It is also linked to another, 'queer' aspect of fungal diversity. The majority of fungi species not only possess both male and female characteristics but also have thousands of different 'sexes', which allow them to reproduce bodies in countless 'post-sexual' forms. This radical proliferation of shifting, sexual multitudes is embraced by post-Internet mutant performers – including myself in my own acts – which helps establish new forms of sociality, or what Donna Haraway has called 'fungal shapes of the queer kin' (Haraway 2008, 10). My work thus positions fungosexuality as a fungal strain of queer identity politics. It entails developing polymorphous and pluralistic strategies for post-sexual body reshapings and replications, in an intimate alliance with the Internet and beyond it.

In what follows, I develop a scaffolding for the concept of fungosexuality in humans by looking at a variety of post-Internet performers in the context of bioart, body art, anatomical anti-dance 'butoh', as well as my own performance practice that was developed from my living experience within London urban decay. My method hinges on a theoretical interrogation of all those forms of bodily performance as anchored in the contemporary philosophies of dark materialism, posthumanism and media theory. The philosophical perspective that emerges from the theories under examination is necessary for establishing an understanding of the mediations of human bodies on the Internet in terms of generative life processes. This understanding of media and life serves as the general philosophical background against which my mutant performance practice unfolds.

How does life manifest itself to us? And what can be learned from the spittle of saliva or the dirt under a toenail in the age of the Anthropocene, when life finds itself under increasing threat? I propose that, to engage philosophically with the world as a biosphere operating on different scales is to 'redeem crude matter' (Zylinska 2014, 111) as it presents itself in seemingly inconspicuous phenomena, such as saliva and dirt, via the theoretical framework of 'new materialism'. This approach endows all forms of matter, including primary ones, with meaningful vitality and agency. As Jane Bennett points out in her book *Vibrant Matter* (2010), even the most elusive material entities have to be considered not as passive background to human activities but rather as influential actants. The living tissue of planet Earth consists of myriads of microbial evolutions, which express themselves globally as the mycelial body (Stamets 2005). Mycelium is the hyper-microbial fungal body that remains invisible to humans as it spreads underground across spaces bigger than the largest metropolitan areas. It excretes soil that it is buried in, creating the primary food source for forests on Earth (apart from the Sun's light). This makes mycelium a key stage in the essential process of life formation that our planet's ecosystem depends on. The microbiota and the constantly running and spreading mycelium condition the temporary stability of human bodies. They also decompose the human body after its death, with decay being the destiny of every complex organism.

Engaging with media through the concept and matter of fungi, I propose a reading of human technology as a process of breaking down the civilisation-extended human body (McLuhan 2001) in order to reuse its matter for novel mutations – although not seen in terms of evolutionary 'progress' but rather as explorative devolution. Thus, my approach can be described as 'techno-rot sensitive', as it is performed from the position of a techno-mutant who is intent on opening up microbial media embodiments.

As the main strategy of my work, I conceptualise fungal decomposition, or rot, as a performative category within the philosophy of technology. In my theory of fungi media, rot is understood as a cluster of phenomena related to the Internet's undoing of the human body, its collapse, disintegration, dispersion and fractured multiplication, at the intersection of networked communication and biotechnology. The cyber/bio juxtaposition has served as a fertile ground for the Internet-era humanities ever since Donna Haraway's 'A Cyborg Manifesto' (Haraway 1991), published at the dawn of the Internet era. The reading of media through those hybrid biotechnological phenomena exposes the technologies of communication as essentially corporeal processes of the human body. Becoming technological and at the same time reconnecting to its microbial nature, the human body partially ceases to be human, I suggest.

My own practice of bodily performance aims to accentuate the physiological nature of media analysed in the fungi media narrative. Reversing McLuhan's theoretical approach to the human body as being extended by media, I position human bodies as extensions of fungi into media communications. I also explore my fungi-human body through media by interpreting technology as offering a human connection with microbial nature. Thus, alongside the reading of media technologies through the human body, I also aim to foreground the fungal characteristics of media technologies via my performance practice.

Performing Practice

My art practice focuses on the body as the subject of both technological mediation and corporeal mutation. The body of the performer is considered to integrate technologies of communication, as well as the microbial entities that inhabit the performance space. The acts and events embody the notion of the no-longer-human body becoming an open-ended technology of life. The microbe-contaminated space of the squatted sewage that sets the primal conditions for the behaviour of human performers is essential for the acts. Considering that the live performance space has been the main performer in all the events that have taken place there, I conceptualise the Dungeons of Polymorphous Pan not only as a curatorial art project but also as a fungal entity that is a medium of life and a prime companion of humans in the depths of the city sewage.

The presentation of the space itself constitutes an important aspect of my work. It shows the performance of microbes reacting to and influencing a variety of anonymous humanoid body acts, or being contaminated by their remains. In the aesthetics of my events (Chronic Illness 2023), I accentuate the 'natural cataclysms' of massive sewage floods, which have been infusing the space with the infamous 'urban-tropical' climate change throughout the whole history of its current squat occupation. Taking into account the squatters, performers and event participants in the space, all the human body acts have been considered only as a context for the dynamics of the microbial occupants. The presentation of the microbial performance at the Dungeons of Polymorphous Pan exposes its bioactive, urban/environmental, industrial/geological, civilisational/historical as well as 'meteorological' features.

As mentioned above, the videos discussed in this book show two of my own body art projects developed in the Dungeons, i.e., *Synthetic Organs*, a performance act using glands made from rotten materials from the Dungeons, and *Holobiont*, a biomedia act involving projections of deformed body parts on moulds and fungi from the Dungeons. The *Synthetic Organs* act is a bodily performance of hysterical communication with parasitic progeny organs (made out of synthetic materials overgrown with mould). The organs are loosely attached to the naked performer's body and are moved around in close proximity via gestures of contortion, violence, gentleness, embrace, expelling, thrusting, hitting, twisting, or otherwise by employing different strategies for jittery morphing. The organs become defined by the performer's various reactions. They are treated as sickly deformations, tender glands, mother's breasts, swollen genitals, breeding cocoons, disgusting babies, additional limbs, an abnormal rash – if not a violent reaction to the body's ongoing mutations. The actions of the performer are choreographed around a face-sized slimy wound or orifice, ingrown into the wall and dripping with synthetic discharge. The wound-orifice was sculpted into the surface of the Dungeons and treated as a body membrane of a living nonhuman entity. The middle opening of the slit nests materials for the synthetic organs of the performer. Prior to being planted inside the wound-orifice, the materials for the organs had been left rotting in the soil inside the space.

The second project, called *Holobiont*, with a nod to Lynn Margulis (Margulis 2001), examines the relationship of the microbial entities in the Dungeons to impaired human bodily acts. Margulis uses this term to name an ambiguous hybrid assemblage of microbial organisms coexisting and reproducing together. The term 'holobiont' originally describes the evolution of life through the mutation of the entanglement of many species that come together as living networks. Yet I understand it as conveying a queer relation of the human performers' bodies to the performance of the bodily entities of microbes. The term 'queer' is used here in the sense of a biodiverse inclusivity for freak bodies, as recently proposed by Haraway (2016). I also include BDSM practice in this work, following the intuition of Timothy Morton. Morton writes about using fossils for restraint accessories such as hemp ropes or latex, embracing 'that shiny, smooth, beautiful, protective BDSM membrane' for the purposes of 'the soothing survival mode' (Morton 2017, 47). For the work, I filmed the human bodies which had been fragmented by restraint and un-humanised by the objectification of the BDSM practice. I also mutated them by means of video editing and then projected them onto the living microbial entities that had been feeding on the rotten materials in the Dungeons. The selection of microbe-hosting materials includes, but is not limited to, mouldy fabrics, fungi-growing boards, clusters of detritus merged with taxidermised animals, as well as microbial traces of the partially moving bodies of the performers. *Holobiont* also involves projections of the restrained and abjectified bodies of performers, whose body mutations feed the multiple projections of the live space.

Throughout my hybrid work I aim to embody the fungal aspects of the Internet and perform it as a human bodily opening towards nonhuman entities. All the conceptual explorations I pursue in this book are intended as an interrogation of, or even assault on, the humanist understanding of technology. My aim here is to redefine technology as a medium of communication with fungoid decomposers. Reflecting upon a variety of theoretical examinations of the bodily contexts of technology, I'm not so much interested in technological artefacts mediating the corporeal. Instead, I want to explore how humans performatively embody the processes of technological mediation. By searching for the fungal characteristics of media, I also aim to develop an understanding of the post-Internet human, with their mutant body and non-reproductive sexuality, as embedded in fungoid life.

Corporeality Beyond Language

Another way of describing the rationale for my work is as an attempt to understand media through their embeddedness in the bodily performance of humans, a performance that always involves fungoid entities. Merging media theory with performance practice, my approach is inspired by dramaturge and actor Antonin Artaud's idea of writing as the spreading of the fungal body. 'The body's spore-like trace is spread across the written page' (Barber 2013, 7) by Artaud, as noticed by Stephen Barber. As Barber suggests, writing for Artaud 'is physical secreting, both savage and interrogative in its impact; it glances sharply of the body' (7). This bodily perspective towards Artaud's writing has been crucial for the formulation of my approach to studying media. Dealing with concepts and ideas, writing for me is essentially a bodily activity – a gestural compulsion involving a feverish performance of limbic incantations. This is precisely what I mean by the dark-vitalist approach which I have adopted in my work. The key inspiration here comes from Artaud's interpretation of language as a mediation of bodily intensities and from his persistent search for performative forms that could re-embody those intensities. In my work I apply the Artaudian method to interpret the Internet as a mediation of human bodies that can be understood through those bodies' re-embodiment in mutant performance unfolding in actual physical spaces.

At the end of his life, before writing anything, Artaud would perform a routine of incantations with a sharp blade thrust into paper pages of his notebooks, accompanied by pencil incisions and cigarette holes. Writing becomes here a performance of respiration, insertion and ejection, piercing through and abjection of the membrane of the human body – which the written page is for Artaud. My own writing about transgressing Internet culture *beyond* the Internet, and about sexual and bodily transgressions *within* various Internet cultures, follows Artaudian intuition to re-translate the mediation of the body back to the tangibility of bodily performance. Artaud's theatrical emphasis on the gestural part of the process of writing accentuates the limitation of language's ability to penetrate the world, which I apply to frame the Internet simulations of the human body. This approach allows me to shift scholarly attention from human intellectual processes and mediatic abstractions, and back to the embeddedness of those processes in the bodily performances that accompany them.

When applying the Artaudian critique of language abstraction to media research, the understanding of the Internet as fluctuations of immaterial code is revealed to be insufficient. In embracing the physiological context for thought, as well as it being a context for the nonhuman life for human media technologies, communication is conceptualised as a live performance – described, after Artaud, as fragmentary and open-ended 'stuttering' or 'mumbling', always only partly understood and expressed. 'Partial sight and limited voice', to cite Donna Haraway, are employed here 'for the sake of connections and openings' (Haraway 1991, 196). Mycelial agencies moving within and opening new territorial plateaux within my performance space and my writing remain in a shared conversation with all life forms, thus aiming to create what Haraway calls 'the world as a coding trickster with whom we must learn to converse' (Haraway 1991, 201). Indeed, alongside Artaud, Haraway's approach to nonhuman life and technology has been instrumental for my research. Her writings provide an extraordinary inspiration for me because they acknowledge microbes not only as communication partners for humans and a vital context for the civilisation of new media, but also as an essential companion of human becoming.

In Artaud's self-reflective writing, ideas are presented as emerging from the human body in a form of slimy discharge, as sweaty mucus – which is the domain of microbial life. In this vitalist, fluid figuration, he obsessively emphasises the primacy of the body before the word – as well as before the world. This urgency is translated in my book into my method of analysing Internet processes through the bodily performance of post-Internet artists. In this approach both language-based concepts and Internet practices feed on intense bodily performance. Artaud proclaims the violent gesture to be a force of repetition that reinforces the obsessive act of formulating ideas. His method oscillates around the urge to understand culture by interrogating the raw material of the human body. This is also the desire behind my work, which aims to explain Internet culture through bodily performance art. My speculative philosophical writing is thus also part of my practice. It could be said that in this book I not only *comment on* fungi media but also *attempt to perform them conceptually* via a number of theoretical gestures. The aim is to demonstrate some of the ways in which my language struggles with the idea of nonhuman communication, craving to engage with words as persistent physiological processes.

Creating a theoretical blueprint for the visceral performance art of the past century, Artaud was often seen hissing while taking notes and accentuating the reading of his notes with savage screams. Demonfighting, violent gesturing, humming and spitting, which he included during his lectures, are examples of over-expressive performative communication, which is energised by a sense of the self-annihilation of the medium of language in order to create an outlet for raw bodily acts. The mind's information, ideas or 'data might never have existed if the body, which at least sweated them out, had not been there' (Artaud 1965, 99). What is inspiring in Artaud for my approach is his uncompromising urge to re-embody all symbolic mediation and achieve a novel insight into human imagination.

Drawing further inspiration from Artaud, I suggest that, to understand the Internet, we need to examine the intimate acts of performative transmutations of the body of Internet users, as well as various penetrations between their bodies and their media. Artaud concludes his poetic dissection of the body with a realisation that organs and parts 'fasten (human) to the rot of life' (Artaud 1965, 44). His morbid obsession with excremental matter is symbolic of the primordial states of human and nonhuman existence. The creation of worlds and the formulation of words are both equivalent for him to the visceral acts of expulsion by the human body of all the entities that always betray the body. The human body also seems to serve as a mask of nonhuman bodily entities. This obsession introduces the question of microbial organisms that live inside the human body and that create the human from within into his conceptual framework – of which I am making use in my work. The re-embodiment of media in performative encounters with fungal entities is the focus of my study.

Artaud offered an original commentary on the electric media when his written words transformed into screams during the censored radio transmission, 'To Have Done with the Judgement of God' (Artaud 1995), at the very end of his life. His offensive shrieking was a self-proclaimed bestial caricature of language, attacking its preciousness as a meaning-making entity. Artaud wished for his screaming language to turn into a plague, infecting others like a virus through the electric wires and electromagnetic waves of radio transmission. This feverish replication, fragmentation and dispersion into new media would become a strategy for making the world grounded in his body – and not separated from it. He wrote about the world as something not yet created but rather as an ongoing process of bodily transformations – which is the strategy adopted today by many post-Internet mutant performers, including myself. Artaud's vision of the world is that of a wound or orifice, openings which abort humans or even defecate them. The world is also described by him as the bestial mouth or gland that spurts the human body as alien spittle. All of those metaphors and visualisations have helped me develop my own aesthetic in my practice, while also tracing a similarity between his ideas and the imagination of other post-Internet mutant performers, who intertwine networked communication with the poetics of contagion in their acts.

The Theatre of Contagion

Artaud's performance-focused bodily theatre provides a crucial strategy for my approach involving the mediations of human bodies with microbial entities. Artaud's 'Theatre of Contagion' (Artaud 1958) became the key inspiration for my own work, as it explicitly links bodily performativity, together with the body's symbolic or even metaphysical dimensions, to the life processes of microbial entities. By looking at how Artaud conceptually transformed theatre a century ago, I am able to theorise post-Internet performance art practice in its crucial relation to fungoid life.

I would now like to explain the role of the Dungeons space in my performance research – which I conceptualise as an iteration of Artaud's Theatre of Contagion. In his article 'Artaud, Germ Theory, and the Theatre of Contagion' Stanton Garner (2006) interprets the concept of the Theatre of Contagion as an intellectual response to Pasteur's 'Germ Theory' by means of bodily performance. Pasteur offered an explanation of human bodily processes through looking at the activity of fungoids. Bruno Latour notices (Latour 1999) that Pasteur's laboratory experiments with yeast fermentation recognised the fungal bodies of yeast as being predominantly performances. As 'microbial causes for century-old diseases were announced in rapid sequence and in often spectacular manner' (Garner 2006, 5), Pasteur's presentations showed that lab or animal (including human) bodies manifested themselves as part of an operating theatre of microbial performers. Artaud takes Pasteur's realisation even further away from the scientific objectification of living bodies and proposes instead his own microbe-obsessed performative method, a method which addresses human bodies via their microbial intensities (Garner 2006, 11).

Artaud's theatre thus becomes synonymous with infectious disease. The theatre space is rediscovered as a space of contagion while human performers are seen as 'infectiously possessed' (Garner 2006, 9). Artaud is said to have established 'theatre and infectious disease (as) defining metaphors for each other' (3), a proposition which provides his performance theory with a network of metaphors for some novel modes of corporeal interaction. Human bodily performance as conceptualised by Artaud is essentially intended to be an expression, or extension, of the microbial entities that animate human bodies. To illustrate that, during his 'Theatre and the Plague' lecture at the Sorbonne on 6 April 1933, Artaud 'shifted from reading his text to replicating the symptoms of plague through and on his own body' (Garner 2006, 11). I see this performance of microbial agency as an important act which, through its extreme gestures, communicates the principle of mediation as a life-generating process. Here, Artaud's vitalism is distinctly opposed to Pasteur's more instrumental approach to the performativity of living bodies. Artaud challenges the fiction of the 'controlled conditions' of laboratory experiments with microbes and replaces the medical lab with a theatre space of bodily transmutation, where spontaneous generation of life can always emerge from a 'void' (Garner 2006, 11). Transgressive theatre and a dance of new imaginary anatomies as envisioned by Artaud are proclaimed as a manifestation of the agency of microbial entities, mediated by human bodies in a form of performative disease, one that transforms humans into different bodies. This is achieved through the uncoupling of living bodies from rational scientific objectification and the recognition of the generative abilities of random particles of life. This is the recognition I am also adopting as part of my own work.

The Artaudian methodology of bodily contagion justifies the transgression of my theoretical work beyond the textual forms of critical humanities and towards the mutant performance within the fungoid space of the Dungeons. As explained earlier, my performance space of the Dungeons is a squatted 19th century sewage infrastructure in decay. It was built as a direct response to the epidemics of cholera, typhoid and tuberculosis in

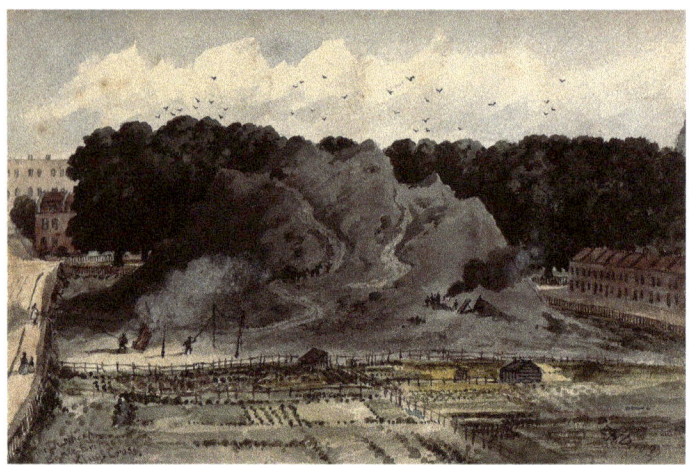

Fig. 4. E. H. Dixon, 1837. *The Great Dust Heap* at Wellcome Collection (Public Domain).

industrial London at the time. As such, it poses critical questions about strategies for living in bio-contaminated, accelerating metropolitan areas. The choice of this environmental context for my practice work was strongly supported by such questions. All urban environments are indebted to microbial decomposers. 'Fossil fuels are a form of necro waste formed from the mainly anaerobic decomposition of buried dead organisms' (Hird 2017, 257), argues Myra Hird. She points out that this is only one of the many ways in which humans use the energy of decomposing microbes to produce their technological infrastructures. Those infrastructures subsequently facilitate the working of the Internet and of other high-tech media. This relationship between microbial decomposition and technological production is of great interest and concern in my work. The material processes that power the most advanced technologies now also make themselves known through the landscapes of growing dumping sites. E. H. Dixon's watercolour painting, *The Great Dust Heap* [fig. 4], from the times of the early industrial development of London, shows an enormous garbage and excrement dump, surrounded by urban slum dwelling and a smallpox hospital in the area. This area is now the North London neighbourhood where the Dungeons of Polymorphous Pan are located, providing an apt setting for post-Internet mutant performance.

Navigating the fungi- and microbe-inspired philosophies of post-Internet mutant performance, the key intention behind this project on fungi media has thus been to create a thought passage to a global environmental imagination from the position of precarious urban living with biowaste. Over the past two centuries of technological development, landfills across the world have grown enormously, as has their biological complexity. As 'landfills assemble billions of heterogenous bacteria' (Hird 2017, 260), the different types of organisms are active in different stages of the processes of waste decomposition, report researchers concerned with nonhuman life. such as Hird. I give them voice in my book because media technologies such as the Internet entail, via their biological energy sources, vast microbial processes that move across the globe as 'leachate', the mixed miscellaneous exhaust of waste decomposition. Leachate 'moves into and through plants, trees, animals, fungi, insects, and the atmosphere. Via leachate, bacteria create well known, little-known, and new biological forms' (Hird 2017, 261). Bacteria also give evidence of microbial intelligence, claims Hird, in the way they develop 'complex and ubiquitous relationality' (261). I consider all those insights about fungoid entanglements with living environments in parallel with the mobility paradigm in global societal processes involved in urban decay. The unknown behaviour of bacteria may have profound consequences for humans who still know very little about them, yet they coexist with them intimately and may be completely dependent on their obscure performance and future mutations. Humans do not understand 'bacterial losses, gains, and transformations, dynamics that are obscured by the scalar mismatch of bacteria and ourselves, by the immensity of their numbers, strangeness of their forms, and the difficulty of accessing many of the environments in which they thrive' (Hird 2017, 261). Dwelling in the architecture of decay, squatters often have to face the problems of environmental waste within urban environments, as they practice living literally within the waste. Mutant performers at the Dungeons fully embrace sewage infrastructures and adopt them as a method of examining the ongoing crisis of human civilisation.

The Re-embodiment of the Digitised Body

For Artaud, the integrity of the human body is bound to be ultimately transgressed into multiple selves in motion. These selves are fragmented and morphing, assuming in the process the shape of phantom limbs which are fighting among themselves. The post-Internet mutant performances that I engage in and curate seek to embody such processes of bodily decomposition through a variety of media. They could thus arguably represent Artaud's intended media presence, such as the radio broadcast that he perceived 'literally to be a physical transmission' (Barber 2013, 164), with the 'scream made new, vivid flesh' (164), multiplying through the electric media of the radio. The immediate and physical transmission serves to intensify Artaud's screaming body, when he proclaims that ideas in themselves are nothing, only corporeal intensity counts as meaningful, as it 'wants to get out'. This ecstatic urge against the dematerialisation of body mediations serves as a manifesto for an impossible dance during his radio transmission, a dance that negates any definite formulation of language or codes.

By developing a parallel between Artaud's concept of the contagious body and the new media context in which it can be productively located, Stephen Barber points out in the chapter 'The Digitised Body of Antonin Artaud' that the mediated body 'remains distinctively extant only in the form of its most obstinate and anomalous residues' (Barber 2013, 231). Barber proposes that Artaud's quest for the immediacy of corporeality finds its unexpected realisation in the mediation of the human body on the Internet and in other new, aka electric, media. Artaud's urge is thus actualised in 'a corporeality enmeshed and disintegrating within digital environments, in perpetual flux, and possessing elements of persistent irreducibility in its most elusive or deviant manifestations' (232). The multitude of mutations was urged by Artaud as a form of a new raw presence of the body, which can be interpreted through Jay Bolter and Richard Grusin's theory of *remediation* (Bolter and Grusin 2000). Their concept describes the twin logic of new media with the complementary categories of *immediacy* and *hypermediacy*. Hypermediacy is the process within mediation that involves a proliferation of the feverish multiplicities of mediated bodies, when at the same time the process of immediacy seeks new forms of the direct presence of the body via mediation techniques. Both processes are intertwined and are remaking each other. Remediation for them involves an attempt on the part of the human body 'both to multiply its media and to erase all traces of mediation: ideally, it wants to erase its media in the very act of multiplying them' (5). For me post-Internet bodily performance is one of the rare human acts that can, actually and materially, *enact remediation*, as it embodies all the multi-mediations of the body in the direct immediacy of the physiological performance of mutation.

Developing a theoretical relation between the Internet and visions of the mutant body in their book *Corpuscular Dawn*, Paul Virilio and Sylvère Lotringer propose that there is a certain symmetry between the manipulation enacted upon the human body by communication media and that enacted by invasive biotechnology. 'The new human of biology corresponds to the cloning of the world itself through the transmission technologies' (Virilio and Lotringer 2002, 102), they suggest. Virilio and Lotringer analyse body art after the Internet. 'Representations of the body, fragmented, abject, grotesque, sublime, monstrous' are for them 'a massive symptom of the body's increasing disappearance' (118) in the advent of technological communications and biotechnology. Performance art indirectly embodies the tendencies of new technologies and the dangerous processes initiated by them – from communication media through to the new eugenics of genetic engineering. The bodily acts of contemporary performers, such as French artist ORLAN, can be seen as reactions against those technological processes. By means of bodily mutilation or abjection, various performances embody the disappearance of the human body in the context of its post-media mutation, as a result of technology entering it. Referenced by Virilio and Lotringer, ORLAN's bodily performances in 1990s (ORLAN 1990) involved or even embraced plastic surgery, in a proclamation of mutant and nomadic identity. Her face was technologically altered in an attempt to go against the ideas of fixed Nature, imprinted DNA or other godly codes programming the human body. The technological processes that facilitated the shifts in ORLAN's identity, such as those related to eugenics and genetic engineering, invade the human body and open it to manipulation within. They redefine the human body as something disposable, made up of multiple misappropriated appearances, and manipulated by the nomadic games of communication entities and media clones of the body itself. This sense of bodily fragmentation and cloning, using technology both as a tool and as a source of its aesthetic, is adopted in my own 'post-Internet' performances in the Dungeons.

Via various mediations, the human body can burst into fragments and find its new anatomy of a thousand forms, at the same time assuming a new intensity of technological presence. This bursting mutation and the new anatomical dynamism are famously called by Artaud the 'body without organs', which is further described in his radio transmission as 'dancing inside out as in the delirium' (Artaud 1995, 307). This delirium nevertheless seems to be infected with microbial bacillus, which animates it into 'a rhythm, which transcends the Dance but seems graphic of Disease' (Artaud 1995, 77). The paralytic shiver, or ecstatic delirium, can be described as the vision of Artaud's electric media that transcends the human body defined by its organs. In many ways this vision has its cruel and dramatic grounding in his experience of having received fifty-two electroshocks in mental asylums. There, the electroshocks served for him as an unwitting performance of the body's decomposition into electric media, resulting in the aforementioned artificial death. He describes the experience in his painful testimonies: 'Thus, wrung out and twisted, finer on finer, I felt myself to be the hideous corridor of an impossible convolution. And I know not what suspension of the void invaded me with its gaping blind spots, but I was that void, and in suspension, ... I was nothing more than a spasm among several chokings' (Artaud 1965, 182).

The violence of such crude technology applied to Artaud's body ended up enacting a grotesque form of a new human corporeality that became his ultimate obsession. The bundle of spasms and choking suspended within a void tragically revealed the rawness of the intense bodily experience that he went on to recount numerous times in his writings. Searching for new impossible anatomies, negating both language and image, Artaud would express in his notebooks a desire for radical nonhuman sexual mutations (Barber 2013, 83) – mutations that could perhaps be seen as technological and/or fungal, as I argue throughout this book. Artaud challenged himself by saying 'it is I who ... tore my body from myself and battle against what is left of it' (Artaud 1965, 187). What seemed left of it, I suggest, was the media proliferation of his body into the residue of microbial performance. The tearing of the mediated body into mutant fragments is similarly being performed by myself and other post-Internet body artists in complicity with fungoids.

I follow the intuition concerning the penetrating agency of media within the human body, by exploring the notion of rot in my narrative about fungi media. I also embody it in my performance art practice, in particular through my acts performed in the self-curated bioactive space of the Dungeons, as well as by involving microbial entities in my acts. Conceptualising my performances, I reference the theories of Artaud, which found their iconic executions in Tatsumi Hijikata's butoh dance performance. Artaud's and Hijikata's transgressive visions and their performances of bodily mutations and surgeries arguably evoke the drama of 21st century media biotechnology, precisely by conceptualising the body as if it was already subjected to the working of genetic engineering or network media communications, reconfigured by the mesh-up of the Internet. Staying in tune with the sense of the diversity of bodily forms is crucial to my work. That's why I have decided to focus on the specific phenomenon of post-Internet performance art, involving practices that not only rework the issues around technological mediations of the human body but also invite reflection on the sustainable relation of technology towards nonhuman life. They do that through staging intimate entanglements with the fungal fabric of life. In this way, they enact post-sexual bodily mutations, which I conceptualise as performative re-embodiments of the bodily mediations unfolding on and 'after' the Internet.

My philosophical reading of performance art, which plays with the aesthetics of androgynous monstrosity or ambiguous anti-sexuality, assigns to it an affirmative value of a novel life pursuit. Importantly, the understanding of life in terms of reproduction through the transformation of bodies beyond the sexual binary, a process I call fungosexuality, is inscribed in the trans, post-sexual or gender-queer character of mutant performances that I observe, research, choreograph and participate in. By researching the post-Internet performance of bodily mutation I thus reconstruct elements of what could be seen as a shift towards an Internet-inspired culture focused on new forms of tangible, bodily participation that celebrates antinatality through non-binary sexualities and nonsexual (although often aesthetically oversexualised) bodily transformations. Importantly, this culture incorporates nonhuman features. The majority of the mutant performers I study and work with identify as queer, trans or fetishist, abandoning heterosexual reproduction and pairing their sexual transgression with the visual dehumanisation of their bodies and the performative expression of intimacy with nonhumans.

Non-normative sexualities are considered in many cultures to be an 'unnatural' degeneration of human life, though through post-Internet body mutant performance they actually build an explicit connection with the environmental concerns which are directly related to the survival of the human species. The emerging sense of queer communality, amongst the multitudes of scattered groups connected by the Internet, not only offers modes of coexistence within radical diversity but also encourages experiments with forms of companionship that are an alternative to childbearing families. What, locally, seems to be an assault on the perpetuation of human life, helps globally to counter the extermination of human living conditions. In this context, I see queer sexualities as offering a cultural decomposition of the accelerated sexual production of humans. For the latter post-Internet mutant bodily performance offers an explicit shift of human sexuality towards a curious and intimate coexistence with non-human bodies.

In order to build my theory of fungosexuality I draw on a variety of resources and conceptual materials in the three chapters that follow. Chapter 2 explores the grounding theoretical landscape of transhumanist philosophies and the critical humanist interpretation of the key bioscience concepts related to fungal decomposition, which my book is inspired by. This exploration facilitates the understanding of human bodily mediations on the Internet in terms of nonhuman life processes embedded in fungoid environments. With an aim to offer a tangible grip on the philosophical problem of fungi media, Chapter 3 focuses on the phenomenon of mutant performance art at the Dungeons of Polymorphous Pan, which has served as a performance space for my work. As my performance practice examines the body of the human performer through its relationship within the fungi-inhabited entity of a live performance space, I draw on texts pertaining to transcorporeality, involving the disintegration of the human bodily form through illness and urban decay. Chapter 4 references a plethora of vivid examples involving online mutant performers who take their practice beyond the Internet through their remediation of bodily acts that seek an intimacy with fungoid life. Literature analysing bioart, queer sexuality, fetishism and biotechnology becomes instrumental to formulating my conclusion about the phenomenon of fungosexuality.

CHAPTER 2

Fungoid Decomposition as a Form of Post-Internet Biomediation

The Contaminated Elements of the Biosphere (aka 'Planet Rot')

This chapter engages with contemporary philosophical theories that account for the transformation of human bodies through media. I discuss them in conjunction with theories of non-human living environments, by way of providing a context to technological mediations. I draw on those theories in an attempt to understand the performative mutations of bodies in post-Internet performance art, i.e., performance art unfolding both in real and virtual spaces but shaped by a specific Internet aesthetics. Post-Internet bodily mutations occurring in these performances remediate the digital mediation of human bodies. My focus is on those forms of bodily performance that embrace fungoid decomposition. I am particularly interested in exploring ways in which such performances account for the ecological entanglement of human and nonhuman bodies – and for the extension of human bodies by and through the Internet. In my 'fungal' take on eco-philosophy (in its 'dark' vitalist guises), I look at decomposition as the key process involved in the nourishment, creation and transformation of living bodies and, particularly, human bodies extended by the Internet. I argue that the mutant performance, which I study in my work, critically reworks the purely biological idea of decomposition by remediating it as technological. The concept of fungoid decomposition, which becomes a media concept in this framework, is understood here as referring to the constitution of the mutant bodies of post-Internet performers. This concept allows me to position performance art as an embodied mode of speculation about human and nonhuman life – and about its technological mediations. This chapter thus outlines several structuring concepts of my 'fungal media' figuration, while preparing the ground for the discussion of fungoid bodily performance in chapter 3, and of fungosexuality in chapter 4.

The pre-industrial definition of media links communication technologies with natural elements. John Durham Peters recalls 'the elemental legacy of the media concept' (Peters 2015, 2) that he traces back to the origins of the philosophy of matter. He argues that media should not be primarily seen as message-bearing human institutions or communication technologies, but rather as beyond-human 'vessels and environments, containers of possibility that anchor our existence and make what we are doing possible' (Peters 2015, 2). In order to understand media Peters urges us to explore nature, positioned as 'the background to all possible meaning' (2). Water, air, earth and other communication channels of the biosphere facilitate life's dynamics. As far as these classical elements are concerned, fungi can be recognised as creators of the earthy composition of the world. Soil, which is a chthonic source of creation for farming cultures, is actually a product of fungi metabolism – it is their excrement. Thus, one of the natural elements identified by Peters as media in fact functions as a seed, or rather as spores of the biological organisation on planet Earth. Interestingly, in Peters' perspective on the 21st century communication networks, those natural elements are described as evolutionary technological infrastructures for the human species. Cultures, being the reworking of nature through technologies, are regulated by media infrastructures that are derived from elements of nature. This process, fuelled and fed by fungal decomposition, provides material for food and microbial energy sources, such as oil or soil. The body of fungi, called mycelium, produces the soil environment that functions as a channel for the biochemical information and energy transfer of plants. Planet Earth is in fact Planet Rot, a fungoid excremental phenomenon that sprouts the most complex life forms, including humans, and it is precisely this fungal element that makes media biologically charged.

Technological infrastructures are shaped by geological formations, argues Peters by describing how those infrastructures reenact atmospheric processes and how they shift with ocean tides. They also use fossilised bioforms that originally captured the energy of the Sun. As Peters points out in his landscape-based concept of infrastructures, media entail not only the human manipulation of nature but also the nature that precedes humans. Thus, the remaking of humans through media is driven by natural elements that go beyond the human. Humans engage with the elements of life to cultivate it – thus starting the civilisation of human cultures – and, in the process, reinventing life technologically. Observing the becoming of technology in human ideas about nature, the fungal perspective can offer us a theory of contaminated natural elements. Media elements cannot be objectified as abiotic abstractions of philosophical substances. Rather, they contaminate each other with infectious strategies of decomposition, as the distinctions between the elements are incidental to their rot-induced mergence.

Decomposition moves all media elements into a fungal bodily expansion. As Paul Stamets (2005) advises in his instructions on farming fungi, mycelia cannot stay alive if they are not moving. Yet fungal body movement cannot be accurately described in terms of the mechanics of the complex structures of animalistic humanoids, as there are too many elusive micro-mechanisms of vegetative movement to comprehend. The movements emerge as forms of blob behaviour. Morphing the blob mass, fungi move by constantly expanding their hyper-cellular body (a body that lacks firm separation between the cells, which is a characteristic of animal and plant organisms) by accelerating the extensions of the hyper-cell. They do not move their bodies as such, but rather change shape through strategies that involve the forking of the nano-tubes they are made of, and by hyper-layering their extended sub-structures that connect and reconnect within. While spreading, fungi feed on many complex bodies – living, dead and in various stages in-between – thus creating a fertile environment for all the complex organisms on our planet. They accelerate the bio-potency of microbial life, enlarging it into the macroscopic form of life that is perceivable to the human eye. They do so by feeding on the decayed carcasses of multicellular organisms of plants and animals, at the same time utilising their most toxic waste. Fungi animate nature's energy loops, before any discrete elements of nature's compositions can be conceptualised, because all the compositional elements of life need the cycles of decomposition to be actuated. The decomposition of fungi media creates a rotting environment full of elements that escape human perception – and that are perhaps too multiple and too dynamic to be charted or represented by precise numerical values of human technologies. As a result, the dirt of decomposing ecologies unveils a complexity that does not fit into the ontologies of wholeness or unity. The concept of decomposition, which I will be drawing on further in chapter 4, has been embraced by many post-Internet mutant performers (including myself). Our performance acts incorporate features of nonhuman species in our use of twisted body expression and forced restraint of movements, latex deformities, rotten makeup, synthetic illness symptoms, fantasy prosthetics, monstrous glands or multiplied folds of fleshy overgrowth.

In his non-hierarchical, pluralistic 'heap' ontology of the biosphere, Timothy Morton defines the category of the 'implosive hole' (Morton 2017, 1), within which entities are related in a non-total, ragged way. 'Holes', as opposed to 'wholes', lack unified structure. They form pluralistic and dynamic connections within life, understood as a multitude of inherently ambiguous processes. Morton describes the biosphere as a set of 'implosive, ultimately meaningless and contingent' (23) symbiotic processes. Based on symbiotic relations, the biosphere has to be ambiguous, as it doesn't specify the dominant body of symbiosis. Morton illustrates this ambiguity with an example of the relationship of humans to microbes inside their bodies. It is not clear if humans are a host *to* microbes, providing a vehicle for them, or if humans are hosted *by* microbes, which perform the essential processes of human life. 'The human body is a hysterical record of nonhuman evolution' (135), adds Morton, by pointing at the nonhuman context of microbial humanity. Both humans and microbes create an implosive whole. Whilst a whole is usually made of the sum of its parts, in Morton's theory of implosion the whole is actually less than its parts but, nevertheless, it offers some form of connection between the parts. Morton proposes that the biosphere and its parts such as ecosystems, species or societies form implosive wholes of heaps. He calls ecosystems 'a heap of lifeforms (and) the biosphere – the heap of heaps' (124). Those heaps are not guarded by general rules that would explain their individual parts. Instead, heaps define certain planes of relationality by allowing for symbiotic mergers. I will show later on how the implosive wholes of the decomposed bodies in mutant performances do not assume any consistent human identity but rather emphasise their relationship to nonhuman life.

In Lynn Margulis' (2001) exploration of microbial endosymbiosis, the evolution of life presents itself as a heap entailing a disproportional complexity. The evolutionary replication of forms is both finite and distorted, as species emerge only at some point in time, change gradually with repeated generational cycles and eventually perish. Any act of reproduction involves random mutation, which means that biological replication involves not only repetition but also change. Moreover, if life unfolds in a dynamic diversity, as Margulis has pointed out, the biosphere cannot be perceived as an organism, as no organism eats its own excrement. Fungi, in turn, do eat the world's excrements, which means that the planetary biosphere as a whole – named 'Gaia' by Margulis – has no integrity that would be similar to human identity or any other form of individuality of a separate bio-organism. Rather, as an entity it relies on fungi to manage its key life processes of waste management. It does not make sense to understand

Gaia as an identity, argues Margulis, while Isabelle Stengers adds that it still may make sense to treat Gaia as one whole, i.e., as a reacting entity, which she calls 'the intrusion of Gaia' (Stengers 2015, 43). Stengers postulates: 'Gaia is ticklish and that is why she must be named as a being' (46) and adds that Gaia does not ask anything of humans because she is not threatened by humans with their technological impact. Gaia's intrusion is careless, as she is 'a ticklish assemblage of forces that are indifferent to our reasons and our project' (47). On the other hand, the 'reasons' for Gaia's 'ticklishness' should be investigated, since humans are threatened by Gaia's reactions to their technological infrastructures and that is the reason for them to consider Gaia as a being. This postulate highlights the connection of human communication technologies to the bio-dimension that precedes humans – and that shall exceed them in the future. Gaia's 'innumerable co-authors, the microorganisms, will effectively continue to participate in her regime of existence, that of a living planet' (47), suggests Stengers. Those microbial agencies, performed by post-Internet mutants, represent a nature that's not innocent, vulnerable or endangered – but that is rather blindly transgressing humanity. Mutant performers enact ambivalence and aesthetically casualise the possibility of self-inflicted extinction. They adopt the perspective of an 'implacable being who is deaf to (human) justification' (Stengers 2015, 47), and who performs extinction beyond any human-centric concern with species preservation.

Fungi are such implacable beings. They enter the human body without notice, in a casual everyday breath, being inhaled in the most basic act of energy sourcing from the environment. Fungi and other microbes always contaminate the air of the earth, challenging the clean distinctions within nature. The separation of natural elements is impossible for fungi media, as nature operates through contamination. Philosopher Reza Negarestani highlights that 'Earth and Water need Menstruum (living mud) to communicate. The living mud is a communicational entity' (Negarestani 2008, 228). The communication processes of life are mediated through dirty contaminations; the earth gets mouldy and moist, the water airs itself into fermentation, the heated air bubbles into boiling pockets of tropical infections and the fire treated by fossilised microbes energises into the mechanical fever of human technology. Fungi media thus melt the natural base-matter into elementary connections of life. Mutant performers engage with the tangibility of those dirty elements and relate to mud, soil and waste, bringing out their own transhuman fertility in the process.

Human Bodies After the Internet

The vital materiality of communication technologies is embedded in the decomposition processes of life. It can be linked to, or studied via, the idea of the death of the Internet. This idea is incorporated by the digital decomposition of human bodies that mutant performance art originates from. Explored by a network of thinkers gathered around the journal *e-flux*, the notion of the decomposition process of media is complementary to the notion of the decomposition of the mediated body through technology. The mediation of the body can be understood as its extension and mutation *into media*. At the same time, the media decompose *into the body* by redefining it in terms of technological performance. Technology is not the end of the body but a pivotal point of its transformation. Hito Steyerl suggests (Steyerl 2015) that the Internet is dead in the sense that it does not work as the late 20th century 'cyberpunk' idea of escaping from the flesh and into a new digital realm. In her account, early 21st century Internet projects go through or into bodies – not only human ones, but also those belonging to the most elusive life forms and environments. Contrary to the cyberpunk utopian ideas of the Internet transgressing the materiality of the body, fungi media transgress the Internet *with* the body, but it is a body that has been technologically decomposed. The corporeal is now embodying the Internet with the diverse performances of fragmentary life entities, with posthuman life embodying new media performance. Steyerl postulates that media technologies and their specific forms of communication are themselves embedded in networked matter. The space of bodily extensions transgresses the technology and becomes a medium *for* technology. Steyerl thus proclaims a return of technology to the flesh. She diagnoses the death of the Internet in its moving 'offline', by noticing that the decomposing Internet becomes greatly intertwined with the bodily entities of 'networked matter' (Steyerl 2015, 17). 'Networked space is itself a medium' (17), she adds, pointing out that bodies outside of the Internet perform as a medium for the Internet in the physical space. Technologies of communication return to the pre-Internet forms of expression that are close to the body, but with the understanding of the type of relationality enfolded by the Internet.

At the beginning of the Internet era in the 1990s, humans who ventured online asked themselves whether they were still human, whilst at the same time trying to define themselves in the context of the new medium (More and More 2013). They were translating their pre-Internet lives into the new medium. Now, after over three decades of the Internet's presence in our lives, humans offline are recognising the patterns of networked media dynamics in the corporeal phenomena. The Internet lives of humans are being translated beyond the medium. Nonhuman and post-Internet bodies, cultures, societies, species, genes, organs, environments – they all perform the corporeal decomposition of the Internet, as the Internet does not merely facilitate the digital translation of bodily processes but is also being incorporated into the bodily dynamics in the way the logic of connectivity is enacted offline. To give an example, Geert Lovink proclaims social media to be an abyss that invades all relations between humans. 'The centre-less network logic comes from media and has penetrated culture in deep way' (Lovink 2016, 190) by amplifying destructive forces in the social organisation and at the same time exposing the fragility behind people's actions. This process is reflected in my performance practice at the Dungeons, 'in which the liquid, the amorphous or the ephemeral overrun both, a characteristic and the subject matter' (Rubel 2012, 94) for the sake of embodying fungoid polymorphology.

In the post-Internet cultures the normalising ideologies of life are dwarfed by life's 'overperformance' by freaks. Zygmunt Bauman describes these phenomena as the attention regime of fluid and mobile images that are less of a structured spectacle but that signal an intensity of a chain of actions. Mutant performance art involves the frailty of body processes, involving 'ephemeral performers and happenings … scrambled together from manifestly and self-consciously perishable materials' (Bauman 2004, 120). The alienation of bodies, cultures, societies, species, genes, organs and environments disperses them into randomised proliferation, as each of those entities becomes reinvented by indeterministic mutations of technologies.

In his essay 'Some Experiments in Art and Politics', Bruno Latour proposes a theory of media-life that merges Peter Sloterdijk's biotech philosophy of 'spheres' with the analysis of networked communications. *Spheres* uses the concept of bodily coexistence, which assumes collective entities of mutation. It presents a variety of theoretical concepts inscribing communication and media technologies within enclosed and compressed tangles and within a dynamics of systemic relations, imagined as forms of bio-capsules. Sloterdijk calls them 'symbolic air-conditioning systems' or 'cultural laboratories to farm humans' (Sloterdijk 2011). Sloterdijk's 'spherical' focus on media exposes different modes of the openness of human identities and of the remaking of the human in the dynamic scenarios of mergence with otherness. Spheres are Sloterdijk's figures of transhuman entities, where human subjectivities are areas on the spheres' surfaces, amorphously defined. Rather than having firm boundaries, they gradually change into not-necessarily-human otherness taking up other areas of a sphere. Spheres are organisational forms of transhuman entities via various media that elude too definite distinctions between human and nonhuman elements, proposing an idea of gradual mergence instead. Latour, in turn, puts 'spherical' concepts of communication within the context of long-distance global processes that distribute spheres disproportionately. He points out that local organisations appear in the context of global randomisation described as 'heterarchy'. 'Local nesting, yes; global hierarchy, no' (Latour 2015, 46) is how he visualises communication networks. This way of thinking offers a structure of the complementary duality of media, which are comprised of both spherical concentrations and dispersions of networks. These spheres, which, according to Latour, are embedded within networks, are anti-essentialist concepts that can account for the ambiguity of transhuman life entities.

The relation of spheres to networks, as described by Latour, maps the phenomenon of the dual functioning of media as immersive simulation environments on the one hand and hypertext interfaces on the other, as argued by Sarah Kember and Joanna Zylinska in their *Life after New Media* (Kember and Zylinska 2012, 131). According to them, a mediated body passes through corporeal networks exceeding the bare presence of interfaces. Encapsulated by the 'framework of immediacy and hypermediacy', this body is 'indicative … of the "double logic" of remediation' (131). Kember and Zylinska borrow the categories of immediacy and hypermediacy from Bolter and Grusin to articulate their concept of remediation (Bolter and Grusin 1998). The hyper-mediated body is a network of affiliations which are constantly shifting. This approach positions the mediated body as interrelated and interconnected. At the same time, the immediacy aspect of remediation immerses the mediated body in an apparently seamless and transparent environment of (mostly graphic) simulations. This dual experience and the dynamic between the two forms accentuate the multiple layers of the remediation process. In mutant performance art, the hypermedial decomposition of the body achieves its novel immediacy via the translation of the body into corporeal acts involving immediate mutations that unfold beyond and outside the Internet.

The Internet itself remains corporeal also because all media simulations and connections are embedded in the materiality of the infrastructural hardware of technology. This becomes apparent especially when the technology turns obsolete. As Garnet Hertz and Jussi Parikka point out in their article about 'zombie media' (Hertz and Parikka 2012), consumption-oriented systems of technology production are driven by strategies of planned obsolescence, which in turn inspire artistic strategies of repurposing the damaged media artefacts. Hertz and Parikka 'believe that media never die: they decay, rot, reform, remix, and get historicised, reinterpreted and collected' (430). Parallel to this narrative of wasted technology unfolds another narrative of waste – Bauman's 'human waste' (Bauman 2004). In *Wasted Lives*, Bauman suggests that, at the beginning of the 21st century, the direct effect of the acceleration of the technosystem involves not only the accumulation of the waste products of industrial production but also the expulsion of obsolete humans, those seen as useless for the global power systems and their technological designs. The 'new fullness of the planet means essentially an acute crisis of the human waste disposal industry' (Bauman 2004, 6) as more people find themselves strategically excluded from high-tech utopias. There is a clear need for decomposing media, feeding on the techno-human waste, and the art of mutant performance provides an enactment of such processes of decomposition.

With this analysis, my fungi media project offers a provocation, entailed in the artistic proposal for repurposing the post-mediated bodies of media users. We know that the infrastructures of human civilisations are made from the decaying bodies of technological artefacts that themselves are constructed from the decaying bodies of prehistoric microbes. Also, human cultures create their symbolic systems out of the dead bodies of past generations. Every aspect of communication thus functions as a mediation of, and mergence with, the dead. By participating in any communication technologies, humans are getting immersed in the decomposition processes of life. Hertz and Parikka point out that 'media cultural objects and information technology have an intimate connection with the soil, the air and nature as a concrete, temporal reality. Just as nature affords the building of information technology – ... so do these devices eventually return to nature' (Hertz and Parikka 2012, 429). And so human bodies, identities, cultures and civilisations decompose through technology, reconnecting again with non-human bodies.

Noticing the base-materiality of media exposes the abstract and rational image of computer networks to be itself a form of decomposition, since every technological refinement is eventually embedded in many raw material temporalities. Digital simulations mask the biological processes that feed them. Recognising the fragmentation of mediated human identities as a form of techno-microbial life reveals the key energetic process of life in decomposition. The infrastructure of body nourishment shares the same digestive system with the decay of excrements. Sexual organs that sprout into the multiplicity of progeny at the same time transmit the deathliest zombie-organisms of viruses and pass on lethal genes. Here, the transhuman bodies of mutant performers remediate the Internet in kinship with fungal life.

The Self-Digestion of Human Bodies Online

As Lynn Margulis reminds us (Margulis and Sagan 2000), human life originated from the mutual cannibalism and incest of bacteria. Both phenomena are common tropes of body horror, referenced by mutant performers through visual forms of auto-consumption and autoeroticism in their acts. Cannibalism involves a body feeding on another body of the same species, it is a devouring of an almost identical body, which is very close to eating itself. As such, cannibalism is symptomatic of the microbial self-digestion of decomposing bodies. Similarly, incest involves a coupling of a body with its own kind, referencing bacteria of the prehistoric proto-species incorporating each other into their bodies. The Internet subcultures of virtual cannibals, like the one analysed by Beth Coleman (2011), can be said to perform extreme versions of the primal auto-consumption desires. Dolcett Internet users, a particular fetish group who offer their cyberspace avatars to be eaten by other users in strangely sexualised rituals, are giving their bodies away to abyssal technonature, where the networks can decompose it with an aid of symbiotic and parasitic simulations. 'Humanity attained such a level of self-alienation, that it can now experience its own destruction as an aesthetic pleasure

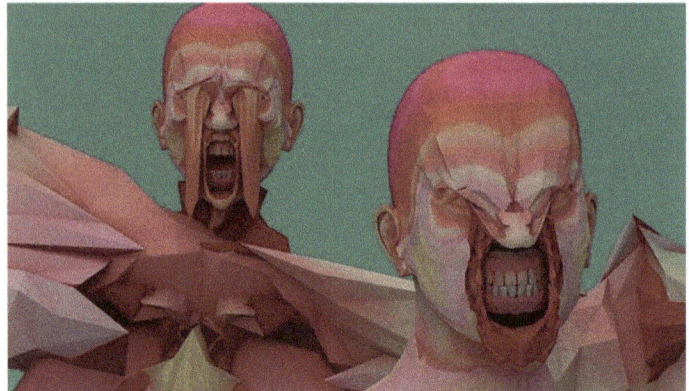

Fig. 5. Mike Pelletier, 2016. Still from *Performance Capture 2*
Image courtesy of the artist.

of the first order' (Virilio 2006, 11), comments Virilio. Media and bodies are feeding on and with each other. Similar visual metaphors reappear more and more often with yet stronger intensities of the aesthetics of bodily implosion in 3D art online.

The *Performance* animations of Mike Pelletier [fig. 5] offer vivid examples of that aesthetics, where technologically-processed human forms collapse into themselves and yet unfold inside-out. Those forms can be perceived as an illustration of a certain abstract technological process, but I would argue that they are not *just* an illustration. Perhaps the general condition of 3D environments already evokes different experimentations with visions of bodily collapse. 3D animated 'performances' visually expose the undoing of the body through media. Also, in these examples, the communication networks turn out to be not only non-linear but also non-surface. Playing with the mushrooming multitude of screen surfaces, fungal media thus operate through networks, deconstructing every image screened by vicious linking, reposting and accelerating network attention, mutating it and connecting with the hidden processing and generating programs or abyssal loop-tunnels. The mirror-illusions of technological interfaces for human bodies disperse them into fragmented fracture-lives. They are networks of undead bodies, which Nick Land calls 'Datacombs' (Land 2010) in his speculative fiction.

Datacombs are the catacombs of databases. Formed by the underground processes of the Internet, they do not organise the world but rather decompose it into a multitude of incomplete carcasses of worldings, by means of involving the digital spaces in the rotting juices of the 'external digestion' of humans by communication technologies. In the narration of *Occultures*, Land describes the outcome of the connection between computer databases and human nervous systems in terms of a delirious, fictional tropical infection. His Internet hallucination reinvents the soft machines of William Burroughs (Burroughs 1992). Soft machines are communication technologies that enter human bodies like junk and dangerously mutate with them. Their codes spread like a virus, deforming human bodies with disproportional organs and breeding the technoid larvae of invisible insects from outer space. They are also related to Burroughs' concept of 'schlupping bodies' that perform 'the total osmotic ingestion or fusion of one body by another' (Kahn 1999, 295). The bodies are staged as a form of biotechnology related to queer sexuality and is later developed into various technological means of bio-communication between human and nonhuman bodies. All those science-fiction figures used by Burroughs and Land are accentuating fungi media performativity, accelerating and spreading human characteristics far beyond the human scale. This contingency of fungi media, which makes a mediated human body behave with an agency of a microbial entity, is encapsulated by Stamets' biomedial illustration of fungal infection within an insect body. The spores enter the body, eating through the exoskeletons and being absorbed via orifices that open the interfaces of the body:

> Other portals of entry include the respiratory tract, anus, and mouth. Once inside, the mycelium forks and runs through the internal organs, interfering with the creature's metabolism and causing malaise, necrosis, and death in a few days. The insects, looking mummified with fuzzy mycelium, then become a launching platform for further sporulation. With some species ..., a tiny club-shaped mushroom ... can sprout from the dead insect carcass. (Stamets 2005, 179)

I would like to accentuate this negative or destructive materialist perspective that fungi media offer, where 'negative' refers to the undoing of the body, which at the same time can be considered 'positive' in terms of entering a new mediatised form of technologically-filtered bodily existence. As post-Internet mutant performers distort their human body shapes by means of digital tools, they achieve novel corporeal forms that invite kinship with nonhuman entities. Focusing on decomposition processes within communication networks brings attention to the base materiality of all cultures, which ultimately consist of human corpses, symbolically mediated into religions, knowledge and history. The death of humans is where the decomposers thrive, opening towards the realm of the microbial, which is where fungal mediations come from. As much as human cultures attempt to repress those processes of decay that fuel life and feed on life, they are themselves essentially grounded in the decomposition of dead human bodies. This is evident in their constant attempts to communicate with distant ancestors, worship totems of ghosts and demons, or perform other rites of magic and religious ceremonies in order to explain the corporeal world. The catacombs are the most ancient remains of human activity, giving evidence of humans' very first attempts to communicate and extend their bodies. Cultures develop as symbolic techniques of the undoing of ancestral dead bodies. Graves and tombs thus serve as the original databases of human civilisation. Humans begin to reflect upon their lives precisely when the life of their bodies ceases to be *human* life. Mutant performers enact this death of (their) humanity via a transgressive experience of bodily mediation, opening their bodies to a thoughtful coexistence with and through nonhuman life.

Slimy Proto-Life Behind the Internet

Ben Woodard's *Slime Dynamics* presents a fertile interrogation of nonhuman media. The metaphysics of organic entities proposed by Woodard (2012a) offers an intriguing example of the posthuman understanding of media, which is arguably one of the most progressive material creations of human thought. In his vision, microbes represent the 'globs of swarming proto-life … that provided the template for all organic beings and all eventual thought on the planet Earth' (Wooard 2012a, 1). Woodard formulates a fungal condition for thought and encourages us to notice the pre-human patterns in the emergence of intelligence. One may even wonder whether humans are not an episodic and pointless addition to the microbial outgrowth. The key point here is the hypothesis about aspects of human intelligence that come from the microbial outgrowth. What is the particular role of fungi media in the microbial claim to human thought? Fungi remake the microbial on a macro-scale, jumping over the gap between microbes and macro-bodies, as Woodward notices. In terms of rescaling nonhuman life for human perception, 'the slime and ooze from which we came is not so unsettling since it appears (for us) as that dead matter which is waiting for potentiation whereas the slime mould, the fungus, appears as the same kind of matter but that which is active of its own accord' (Woodard 2012a, 24). Fungi thus perform as the media of microbial agency, embodying the slimy nonhumans in the human scale. Described by Woodard as 'globs of proto-life', these slimy creatures are embodied in the human scale by both fungi and media technologies. According to Woodard, the microbial dimension of nonhuman life that is most unsettling for human perception is to be found in fungal bodies. Mutant post-Internet performers play with this synchronicity by staging their experience of technological mediation via adopting fungal shapes in their bodies.

The newest media simulations picture the body's collapse in ever more intense renderings. The oddity of virtual worlds, showcased unsettlingly by the sleekness of 3D animations and their glitches, reveals visions of the technological growth of fleshy wastelands on the Internet. Replacing, extending and imploding into human bodies, fungi media thrive on humans and transform them into something yet undefined. The fragmentation of the human body in the luminous reflections of the screens reflects the apparatuses feeding on humans and mushrooming from them: 'The fungal marks the unnerving nature of somatism – the food of the dead and fruiting bodies. Fungal bodies are thus hardly bodies at all as they stretch the conceptual limits of their own bodies as well as destroy and decay the purportedly solidity of other bodies' (Woodard 2012a, 29). The first stage of the decomposition of the body is the auto-cannibalism of cells and fungi, which are the prime agents of decomposition, reminding humans about their conflicted corporeality. It is the creeping life exposed in fungi media that makes human technological bodies amorphous, or makes them appear as performative network variations without form.

Digital mediations of human bodies which inspire post-Internet mutant performers do not emphasise a defined bodily structure which undergoes various life processes, but the processes themselves. The structures of virtual bodies are about slimy shifts of fungi media networking. The processual virtual bodies cross the separation between matter and energy, or body and intensity. They behave like protoplasmic masses that represent a connectivity underlying all life in an exquisite slimy moment. Slime perpetuates the dynamic of extilligence – an intelligence externalised in microbial networking. Networks of microbes become extended through human media technologies that embody the fungal 'external nervous system' analysed by Stamets (2005). The slimy extilligence of fungi media collapses human thought into no-longer-human technological bodies. Human thought reflects itself in fungi media as only one stratum of nature, while technology embodies many natural strata beyond thought. This is why the performativity of media technologies radically transgresses humanist self-reflection.

The question of a radical opening to transhuman life through technology, which post-Internet mutant performances interrogate, was posed by Donna Haraway via her concept of the cyborg. Her postmodern narrative of the 'cyborg myth' unveils the ontology of techno-biological hybrids. The cyborg is resolutely committed to partiality, irony, intimacy and perversity (Haraway 1991, 153). It is a many-headed monster standing against the unity of identity. The cyborg is a coursed beast, an illegitimate offspring, bred from an awkward merging of humans with media technologies. It spreads into invisible omni-potentiality of presence, signalling random multiplicity. An infectious affinity of fragmented identities has the lightness of a puffball, sprayed with facture so fine that we cannot see the very fragments or bits of information. We cannot predict our possibilities. The bestial appearance of unicellular techne once again escapes the framing of the calculated scenarios of the future. Life after media goes beyond the rationale of computing and spills the vulgar leakage of the diversity of chances. The bio-feedback of technologies, understood as their grounding in obscure materialities, embeds them in a randomness of corporeality. The variety of life forms does not make any sense; it is not composing any complete symbolic system, illustrating a plan or copying human intelligence. Evolutionary expression is ridiculous, disproportionate and surprising! I want to suggest that Haraway's cyborg can serve as a figure of fungi media in the sense that it postulates the essential openness of high technologies to even the most awkward mergings with bio-bodies. Fungi are arguably the most elusive living entities, ever confusing the sense of human identity.

Participating in media decomposition, post-Internet performers emerge with various mutant singularities that morph them away from the idea of the 'human species'. Timothy Morton makes a blatant point proclaiming the non-existence of the human species, as techno-humans have to learn to be 'humans without humanity' (Morton 2017, 124). Though looking at the symbiogenetic evolution of life, the kinship of freaks beyond the lineages of species is not unusual at all. 'Bacteria do not have species' (Margulis 2001, 8), writes Lynn Margulis, pointing out that the freak is a rule of microbial life, with no firm separation of bodies and the intense fluidity of bio-cell identities. According to her testimony, genetic research and other biochemical work explore the chimerical nature of life that contains in its forms a variety of unrelated genes in different parts of the same organism as well as allowing seemingly separately defined organic forms to merge with each other. Mutation, reproduction and the reproduction of the mutation of microbes are all embodied in mutant performance.

Microbes within microbes form symbiotic bodies, feeding on each other and reproducing within as part of an elusive amalgam. Mutant performers engage with those processes as they enact the integration of symbiotic bacterial communities that create complex bio-forms. All cells of unicellular organisms come from the mergence of microbes: e.g. 'cells with nuclei originated through a specific sequence of merges of different types of bacteria' (Margulis 2001, 40). Multicellular identities of macroscopic organisms are formed by the incorporation of microbes and their transformation into compound bodies. Technological symbiogenesis can be understood as 'the appearance of new bodies, new organs, new species' (Margulis 2001, 43) through a cohabitation of very different kinds of organisms connected by technological infrastructures. Those forms of new organs and species constitute the narratives of mutant performances. Humans form virtual networks of fungi media, embodying the vast networking of microbes that form the human bodies and bodies of all other organisms that humans can perceive. 'All organisms large enough for us to see are composed of once-independent microbes, teamed up to become larger wholes' (Margulis 2001, 43). Uncovering the microbial past of our bodies, Margulis also stresses the fact that microbes lost some of their individuality in the process of evolution. She then suggests that humans partly give up their individuality in the process of co-emergence with their technologies. Last but not least, human technologies are made from bodies of other living organisms and impact technologically on many more by a thorough interference of human-made infrastructures within the biosphere. This making of humans as living entities of nonhuman humus is accounted for in mutant performance.

Microbial Intelligence, Or the Sophistication of Decomposers

The spectacular exposition and computational recognition of the mediated multitudes of miniature biosphere bodies pressures us to rethink the human body in a radical way. Scanning our planetary bubble of life with contemporary technologies, we are lured to zoom in onto the microbiological level and notice 'life itself as starting from a single cell' (Amato 2000, 100) through the perception of the cellular units of biological organisation. Joseph A. Amato proposes the cellular scale of life as a stage for his media-archaeological narration about 'dust' in the book of the same name. 'The smallest living creatures can undo the greatest' (Amato 2000, 155), he states. Amato sees the story of the human discovery of microbes as a turning point of civilisation, one that eventually inspires the advancement of media technologies and that offers new forms of existence in computer-based virtual realities. Describing human obsession with microbes posing deadly threats to the civilisation of hygiene throughout history, he sees industrial technology as an attempt to tame microbes. Amato suggests that media simulate the microbial dimension of life by reconstructing them as technological processes, and at the same time try to control microbes by replacing them with simulations, thus neutralising them via the distance of technological abstraction. Clean abstractions of corporate and other institutional media environments are clearly an extension of the cultural paranoia of hygiene and of the control of power systems.

A simple constitution of unicellular organisms in critical mass leads to the emergence of an intelligent behaviour of spontaneously made-up dynamic structure, according to theories of bio-emergence proposed by Francisco J. Varela (Varela 1991) and Anthony Trewavas (Trewavas 2014), allegedly exceeding the sophistication of the most advanced computer networks at this time. Also, computer networks amass various processes and activities of human involvement, which exceed centrally-designed algorithms that have been created to regulate them. This is why the Internet or VR systems cannot be perceived only as isolation (Amato 2000, 166) from the 'crude matter' of Amato's dust. Amato does not properly recognise the microbial intelligence and fails to consider the connection between microbes' behaviour and the performance of the remaking of the human species within their technologies. Indeed, he perceives dust as rather crude. Perceiving dust as crude is rather crude itself, as the left-over detritus in the random bio-geological location on our planet (even on the outskirts of the atmosphere) actively partakes in the minuscule microbial life processes on the global scale.

In his concept of 'germs', Amato to a certain extent demonises microbes by referencing systems of social control (eugenics) that create the scare of random mutation and employ technologies to isolate the human species from microbes. He writes: 'Virtual reality is the logical culmination of a society whose members' lives and minds are removed from direct contact with the stuff of the world – its dust and dirt – and are constructed around refinement and manipulation of human and natural environments' (Amato 2000, 166). Although Amato presents media as directly linked to microbes, he positions media as being microbes' antithesis – something that separates humans from the minuscule. Contrary to this perspective, I examine how media actually redefine humans as minuscule processes by connecting their nervous systems to the microbial entities of their bodies, in the most extended sense of the biosphere. Network media such as the Internet are the new dust that is contagious and that sprouts complex viral mutations in the technological extensions of humans. According to Amato's expertise in the history of civilisation, negative tendencies in the cultural perception frameworks stop us from recognising affirmatively the bio-potency of technologies, particularly the life of media. Generally, people tend to only notice the relatively rare life-threatening microbes, while at the same time completely ignoring the majority of microbes that are necessary for sustaining any complex life on planet Earth, including the life of humans. Yet humans tend to demonise the majority of microbes as germs, perceiving them solely as the origin of diseases while forgetting about their crucial role in the biosphere. Paranoid repulsion from life tends to reduce the network behaviour of ambiguous symbiotic relations to 'a complete narrative of contagion, epidemic and plague' (Amato 2000, 166). Thus, popular understanding commonly identifies microbes, such as fungi, as a life threat.

To counter this antagonising attitude towards, and alienation from, the microbial fabric of life, mutant performers engage with a counter-perception that explores the embodying of the microbial organisation in media as a more sophisticated form of engagement with technology. This form of engagement happens through establishing technological participation in microbial life. Media technology performs as a residue of invisible life processes. Fungi and viruses have played a key role in the emergence of the whole of multicellular life on the Earth, employing direct slitting mechanisms into DNA. The evolution of species is submerged in the microbial networks of 'great evolutionary forces, such as symbiosis and hybridization, (which) are of a vital importance' (Ryan 2009, 5). Frank Ryan in his theory of virolution introduces 'a very different perspective of evolution than selection working on informationless noise' (Ryan 2009, 5). Microbes act beyond natural selection and random mutation as they perform 'natural genetic engineering' (a paradoxical term in itself) by transferring key genes between the nuclei of plant and animal cells. Thus, germ theory is one-sided at best and actually conceptualises technologically-conceived scenarios of extinction, as exterminating microbes (i.e., total hygiene) would equal the extermination of the whole of life as we know it on our planet. But technology is unable to kill all life. Even if it seemingly changes a great deal for humans, it is still not really threatening for miniscule life. Even the most dystopian visions of the technological suicide of human civilisation cannot convincingly conceptualise the death of bacteria. On the other hand, perhaps human technologies that make up civilisations can survive or even thrive by learning from microbial networks.

The scale of the human body and human perception, with its pace aligned biochemically with the pace of animalistic movement, made classic theories of evolution emphasise violent competition for sexual partners (Darwin 1861). The valid expressions of life's intelligence according to those evolutionary mechanisms of sexual violence are mostly actions that are proportionate to animalistic moves, perceived as a decisive factor if a mutation is to occur (e.g., competition for a sexual mate). Similarly, perspectives on life processes completely ignore the microbial networks that create the fabric of the entangled web of interactive mutations. Thus, Amato argues that 'human imagination will not be transformed by the microworlds of science and technology' (Amato 2000, 175) because the scale of human bodies makes microbes meaningless for humans. In his summary, Amato suspects that the hyper-complex multicellular organisation of human bodies makes us unable to relate to microbes, or at least does not allow for an appropriate account of the miniscule scale. Yet the fact of the matter is that microbiota actually regulate the key human bodily processes, from sex and digestion through to mental and other chronic illnesses. In its essential functioning, human bodies actually *are* microbial. Even the nervous system apparently behaves like mycelium and can be drastically influenced by various biochemicals sourced from fungi. To recognise it, one has to imagine the miniscule movements caused by non-centralised nervous cell entities (of microbes, fungi or plants) in their most radical consequences of body mutations, embodied and enacted by post-Internet performers.

When it comes to understanding the relationship between human and nonhuman entities, the work of Anthony Trewavas challenges humanist common sense. In his book *Plant Behaviour and Intelligence* (2014) Trewavas aims at defining the intelligence of life forms beyond anthropomorphic thinking and its animalistic perception – and instead recognising intelligence in the behaviour of plants as well as microbes and fungi. Trewavas writes that the human understanding of intelligence is an 'anthropic or anthropomorphic supposition' (Trewavas 2014, 14). In his view, humans impose their expectations about what qualifies as intelligence based on how they can perceive behaviour. Fungi behaviour is hardly perceivable for humans and thus fungi as well as other microbes are not recognised as intelligent by us. At the same time media technologies mimic the behaviour of microbial entities for human perception and are recognised by humans as intelligent. Microbes and plants do not move at a pace recognised by human perception and have no defined nervous systems, though isolated nerve cells of plants behave indistinguishably from those of animal nerves, throughout the long series of parallel variants of conditions. The difference is made by the complex organisation of animal nervous systems – in particular, by the human brain. The brain's cognitive functions are linked to the pace of movement as defined by the speed of communication between nerve cells. Trewavas concludes that 'most animals that use nervous systems for communication will operate their movements on a timescale familiar to ourselves' (16) because the pace of communication within all animal nervous systems, as well as the body coordination of animals, have similar speed to human bodies and brains.

Trewavas shows that brains are not necessary for intelligence, taking an example of the slime mould that learns about its environment and changes behaviour in reaction to this environment (as evident, for example, in its discrimination between food sources). 'This single-celled organism is therefore capable of simple reasoning' (16). Intelligence is defined by Trewavas as a process beyond cognition and is understood as adaptation of highly organised and centralised nervous systems. Deconstructing the brain, Trewavas recognises intelligence on a cellular level and in the self-organisational abilities of the multitudes of separate living cells, such as microbes. Communication between common bacteria illustrates the decomposed microbial intelligence that media embody, breaking down the functions of the human brain into technological extensions, which drive its behaviour with the intelligence of media networking. Trewavas argues:

> [V]arious signal transduction assessments show the intelligence of bacteria. Bacterial communication is apparently meaning-based and permitting colonial identity, intentional behaviour (e.g. pheromone-based courtship for mating), purposeful alteration of colony structure (e.g. formation of fruiting bodies), decision making (e.g. sporulation), and recognition and

identification of other colonies, are credited with and resulting from a bacterial social intelligence and wisdom. (201)

It is the volume of microbial entities that accompanies their structural reorganisation. Unicellular organisms' simple rules or basic elements in extreme number inspire the bottom-up emergence of the complex structural dynamics of entities such as hyper-microbial mycelia that regulate the biosphere. Microbes form the network media of mycelial bodies and bacterial symbiosis, structures which are similar to the computer networks of the Internet. Those networks have many elements with a few connections (so-called connectors) and only a few elements with a lot of connections (hubs). These processes of networking are related not only to emergence but also to 'stigmergy' – the control of the structure by information that comes from the structure itself. It is the rewriting of the behavioural patterns based on previous behaviour that humans teach their 'intelligent' media.

A famous illustration of the narrow and mechanistic understanding of intelligence is the ability to navigate the maze – performed by slime moulds as well as computer game players. The navigation of the maze seems to be a task that clearly evaluates the decisions as intelligent on a scale of basic efficiency. The ability to navigate not only serves as recognition of the intelligence of microbes but also exposes the part of human intelligence that is shared with microbes. Interestingly, Trewavas mentions 'the ability to navigate a maze (that) is shared between social insects and plants' (99), where the 'maze' is understood as soil and air – which are the excrement of fungal and microbial digestion. Fungi decomposition provides therefore the environment in which microbe intelligence is performed. Every unicellular organism 'gathers and continually updates diverse information about its surroundings, combines this with information about its internal state, and makes decisions that reconcile its well-being with the environment' (Trewavas 2014, 100). Some cognitive scientists, e.g., Varela (1991), would recognise those patterns as characteristic of the cognitive processes of the human brain. To recognise those feedback patterns of behaviour in microbiological bodies, thanks to the observation done with apparatuses of human technology (i.e., human bodily extensions), constitutes a technological opening of humans towards the miniscule media of microbes. The technological networks are filters through which human life presents itself to human perception as microbial processes. Technological mediation constitutes transhuman life. We perceive our techno-bodies as media-microbes, since the technologies expose and increasingly emphasise the processes of human functioning as dependent on microbial life.

Stamets repeats the argument, originally made by Lynn Margulis, that symbiosis is not an exception in nature but rather the norm. The advantage of recognising the fungal media realm of intricate microbe communication networks can be of much greater importance than the threats posed by infectious parasites. Anna Tsing's narration about 'the mushroom at the end of the world' (Tsing 2015) shows how fungal strategies can lead humans beyond the self-inflicted scenarios of technological disasters. In her story the 'capitalist ruin' of abandoned US industrial sites sprouts Japanese mushrooms that provide food, jobs and new lifestyles for the excluded, globally dislocated populations of the 21st century. These populations negotiate their life with fungi that become the environmental media of post-industrial, dynamic social networks. The mushrooms at the end of the world are a fine example of fungi media for a future remediation of environments and communications. They perform parasitic and infectious processes, but their context goes far beyond that. 'After hundreds of millions of years of evolution, fungal alliances have become part of nature's body politic. It is time for our species to partake in this ancient mycological wisdom' (Stamets 2005, 34). Stamets urges us to take an active part in what he calls 'Mycotopia' – an environment in which fungi are actively used to enhance or preserve an ecological equilibrium. Certainly, the fungal behaviour eludes the imagination of proportionate balance as it spreads by deforming the environment into overly complicated and patchy holographic discontinuities. Then, certain technological involvements with the biosphere can be considered advantageous or disadvantageous from the perspective of human survival on the planet. How can fungi media possibly enhance and preserve human environments? In describing his theoretical 'Mycelial

Internet' Stamets lists the following advantages for the dynamic functioning of the biosphere: enabling greater nutrient flows, improving moisture absorption, bolstering disease resistance, reducing erosion, providing niches for fauna and flora, and bequeathing debris streams for more fungal cycles. He argues that future habitat restoration has to be founded on 'three systems – mycorestoration, permaculture, and living machines' (Stamets 2005, 68). Decomposition finds its meaning through novel lifestyles that answer the problems created by global technological civilisation.

Taking distance from the face-value of Stamets' somewhat naïve enthusiasm about 'perfecting' the future of humans with mycoremediation, let us explore the notion of decomposition media that he promotes as a future approach to technology, beyond the reckless push for production and consumption. Fungi media can be seen as the opening of technological modes of existence beyond the market. Those intriguing 'living-oriented' modes of fungi media are described with terms taken from other theorists of ecosystems. The 'living machines' of John Todd describe mycelial networks that break down toxic waste (as in estuary ecosystems) while the 'permaculture' of Bill Mollison describes the strengthening of the sustainability of an ecosystem by using diverse natural systems, which are also regulated by fungi. Stamets' own 'mycofiltration' references both of the above-mentioned ideas by describing the diversity of specifically applied mycelial filters. Fungi media also perform as filters, but these are filters created by humans for the human perception of reality. They showcase the miniscule life we couldn't perceive before the technological apparatus, and thus completely change our relation to the world. They also challenge the hyper-structure of our supposedly essential multicellular integrity and introduce the microbiological diversity with their minute temporary performativities.

Within their microbe scales, fungi media undo human identities through the decomposition of network communication and the fragmentation and external digestion of immersive simulations. Medial decomposition then embeds the no-longer-humans in the cryptic materiality of anonymous substances, revealing the slime dynamics behind intelligent behaviour. This post-technological, microbial embodiment of intelligence defines us through nonhuman modes of performativity with fungi, slime moulds and other mysterious microbes. My aim here is to have a closer look at that process as it unfolds within decaying urban spaces and post-industrial areas. The bioremediation of fungi introduces the media of bio-agency that alter the never clean but technologically altered environment through openings towards contamination and through undetermined compositional shifts. 'The introduction of a single fungus ... into a nearly lifeless landscape triggers a cascade of activity by other organisms' (Stamets 2005, 69). By entering habitats, fungi tend to remove toxic barriers for synergistic waves of organisms to follow. Fungi media lead the change of environmental biotechnologies. They decontaminate land not by sterile instrumentation of control but rather by loosening it up and opening it to the self-regulating sophistication of dirt. Pre-exposed to wild bacteria, mycelium grows more vigorously, while other groups of bacteria produce their own toxin-digesting strategies and proliferate with fungi media. The chain effects of communication technologies' processes inspire arrays of new media enclaves, which are full of tech-mutations that are ready to descend into the hidden sub-territories of loopy interfaces and decaying metropolitan environments. This movement beyond the Internet and towards biodeteriorated urban spaces may be the most vital opportunity for the fungal understanding of media.

The Human Body, Extended and Decomposed

Post-Internet mutant performers tap into the conceptual perspective of Virilio and Lotringer, who position the technologically decomposed body of the human as a new corpuscular form of existence, or a novel materiality of life. They present a vision of the devolution of the human via post-industrial technologies, performed by a collapse of the body. Virilio and Lotringer's concept of media mutation does not usher in any productivist evolutionary ideas but rather serves as a conceptual opening to the notion of the devolution of techno-rot. In their proposition 'everything decomposes because of the acceleration of exchange, the deconstruction of instances and of institutions' (Virilio and Lotringer 2002, 164). Linear notions of the future and of progress are rejected here with the shift towards the post-structural dynamics of technological acceleration, which has been fast-forwarded by the Internet.

The acceleration of decomposition eludes the future-oriented ideologies of progress, moving (backwards) towards the microbial past. Virilio and Lotringer conceptualise this process as the 'regression of matter', which not only involves 'social decomposition in the cities, decomposition of the social fabric into anomy' but which also affects human reality in the most abstract as well as in its physiological dimensions: 'What is decomposing is the geographical space, the psychophysical and the "psychophysiophysical" space of being' (165). In their multi-layered narrative, which offers novel technological understandings of the human body, Virilio and Lotringer thus establish *decomposition* as the key category to conceptualise the process of corporeal erosion that accompanies the different processes of mediation. They mention the loosening of the integrity of nation state politics as a result of the postcolonial flux of transmigration and the globalisation of economy. They relate the above to the loosening of the stability of social hierarchies affected by the higher social mobility enabled by new communication media. Last but not least, they focus on bodily erosion performed by biotechnologies such as genetic engineering, alongside the diversification of cybersex and gender-fluid tendencies of humans in the highly mediatised environments. Virilio and Lotringer extend their understanding of the human body beyond the body proper (also called *animal body*), and beyond the social bodily organism, into what they call the *territorial body*. The territorial body is the ever-encompassing historical relation of human civilisation to its environment. This relation redefines the environment and at the same time defines the human body as technologically extended. The integrity of the body is being challenged here. The erosion of the territorial body happens through disconnection from the land, by loosening human dependency on their location. It also happens through processes and phenomena such as globalisation, living in megacities and smart apartments. Global mobility, urban alienation and high-tech separation inside the simulation chambers of 21st century apartments pressurise humans further into joining media communication networks as the main context for their self-definition, which accelerates the processes of the media decomposition of human bodies and subjectivities.

Various definitions of the human body explored by Virilio and Lotringer overlap with each other in a monstrous tangle which is almost nonhuman, constantly morphing. The two authors elaborate on the erosion of those definitions, describing 'the decomposing social body, where structures of procreation, of production, and of course of resistance in any area are themselves unsettled' (166). In their analysis of techno-human bodily dysmorphia, Virilio and Lotringer adopt a global perspective by suggesting that the planet's territory becomes increasingly subjected to technological manipulation and thus functions as the human's extended body. The collapse of the territorial body into the human body proper makes 'The Earth (its) phantom limb' (Virilio 2000, 18), adds Virilio, as the whole planet seemingly performs as a technological bodily part of humans, mediated by global communications. We could thus say that communication technologies internalise our planet as a collective of bodily functions in the embrace of the processes of mediation. The planet in its entirety is involved in the physiological processes of the techno-human body, extended by the global infrastructures. In Virilio and Lotringer's argument, technological networks infiltrate not only humans but also the whole living surface of the planet. The performances of human bodily mutations that I engage in and curate can thus be seen as commentaries on global environmental changes.

The human usage of technology alters life on our planet through the extreme manipulation of the environment and its energetic metabolism. Taking the example of carbon cycles as the major rhythm of the ecosystem, technological bodily extensions of the human – such as industrial infrastructures, metropolitan areas and transportation vehicles – work as 'energetic slaves' that consume several times more energy (probably more than five times, a number estimated by Volk in 2003) than humans themselves. 'We nourish these energy slaves with the remains of ancient life' (Volk 2003, 55). We could suggest that humans breed into a new species through their bodily media. Those new forms of technolife are very demanding towards all other life forms, especially primitive ones. Energy-expensive media technologies, feeding on the prehistoric microbial heritage of the Earth, decompose the pre-industrial forms of the biosphere (petroleum) and mutate humans into the techno-environments of their many infrastructures navigated by the Internet and other global computer networks, which humans are so dependent on and overwhelmed by. Humans are thus being actively redefined by media technologies that change their body – and that actually become their body.

The architecture of networked communications grows from the agglomerations of urban landscapes. Cities are often built over graveyards and are embedded in them, containing a decaying hollowness within them. In one of the subchapters of his study of fungi, Stamets comments on urbanisation with the description of the 'house wrecking' fungi that break down toxic waste (Stamets 2005, 90). At first fungi perform as an enemy problem destroying human cities, but at the same time they neutralise the global-scale side effects of metropolitan industries. Urban decay is reinvented by fungi as an opening for techno-mutations. Mouldy skyscrapers are the new ground of fungal metabolism, as they reintroduce the uncertainty of microbial life into the high-tech control system that is obsessed with cleanness and hygiene. In this post-apocalyptic setting of decaying architecture, mushrooms that grow in abandoned industrial spaces promise a new form of life's organisation.

Unfolding his ideas about 'mycoremediation', Stamets calls for the fungal undoing of urban industries by offering new bio-designs that are inspired by the many roles played by fungi in the biosphere. One of his campaigns, the mycoremediation of forest roads, inspires a different way of thinking about the transportation channels of communication. It offers a narration about the revitalisation of communication environments through microbial contamination as opposed to stories of bioterror, in which global microbes' travels spread deadly diseases. Mycoremediation rethinks human communication with microbes, developing sophisticated co-relation channels beyond basic parasitic contaminations. Symbiotic strategies for fungal life go beyond the model of abusive invasions of war machines and towards the idea of the nourishing interdependence of civilisations. Civilisations have always been mediated by transportation infrastructures – fermenting canals irrigation, roads marked with symbolic stones, rail tracks with underground arches of tunnels and bridges, radioactive airplane corridors, deep pressure oceanic capsules, bike lanes (McLuhan 2001). As Haraway notes in her 'Cyborg Manifesto' (Haraway 1991), tourism has become one of the world's largest industries. Various postmodern travel lifestyles, which Bauman calls 'liquid' (Bauman 2000), can actually be cheaper than stationary accommodation. Many IT experts live lives of nomadic postcolonialism. Redundancy and the screen sterilisation of information society jobs stimulate the increase in media portability.

Consumerism replaces work partially with the playful homework of private time and entertainment. The pressure of mobility causes stress and requires the remediation technologies of coping with the jamming of loopy networks. Haraway recognises this situation as a side effect of the disturbance of overcoming the futurist militaristic media called 'C^{3}I' – which stands for command, control, communication and intelligence. Indeed, the military developed the network media prototype of the Internet, which turned into the transpolitical bubbles of virtual subcultures. 'Weaving' is proposed by Haraway as a subversive cyborgic form of networking, actualised through polymorph storytelling against the domination of singularity. Her heretical 'heteroglossia' is the choice of struggle against the universal code and the standardised modes of communication. Military control is distanced in the trance-state experience of connected computer users, their webs of new couplings and new coalitions.

The late-20th century utopian desire of and for the Internet is reformulated by Haraway in the early 21st century in her book *Staying with the Trouble,* by returning to the fleshy temporality of the cyborg bodies as a point of focus. To recapitulate, the post-futurist cyborg thrives with the multiplicity of creatures – the techno-alien life forms that are not reducible to each other but that are morphing together, propelled by their lack of firm bodily boundaries as well as their frayed digital insubstantiality. At the same time, the cyborg is recognised as a symbiotic biological entity, linked to specific time-space positioning. 'Nobody lives everywhere; everybody lives somewhere. Nothing is connected to everything, everything is connected to something' (Haraway 1991, 31). The dispersion of the selves of online humans accelerates with the infectious strategies for survival in urban diasporas and their particular conditions. The entanglement of global urban-nomadic lifestyles speeds up with cheap travel infrastructures and social media networks, but retains its histories and disproportional conditioning. In order to examine this entanglement, I offer an account of my own urban and media nomadism in Chapter 3, via my research involved with squatting networks in London.

The decomposing ambience of rotting architecture is being uncovered by the archaeologies of postcolonialism. It is also a process of collapsing the old global empires and internalising their previously expansive dynamic, summarised by Ben Woodard in the context of slimy microbial life as an 'ongoing slumification and slime-ification of the capitalized earth' (Woodard 2012a, 94). Juan Carlos Rodriguez describes the fungal rot of the Cuban Revolution film archives as an invasion of nonhuman agency against the ideology of urban modernisation. He notices that microbes not only invade the physical city but also eventually devour media infrastructures. Both processes are parallel and mutually related, as city 'ruins belong to the same history of abandonment and oblivion as those images infected by fungi' (Rodriguez 2018, 172). The ideology of urban design is being challenged by biodeterioration as 'toxic biological agents such as fungi and bacteria colonise and contaminate archival images of social transformation and revolutionary processes' (Rodriguez 2018, 173). Another example of biodeterioration can be analysed through an inverse shift in the meaning of the term 'squatter', applied nowadays to describe 'makeshift urbanism' (Vasudevan 2017, 146) with its 'micro politics of violence'. The settlers of the British Empire, violently claiming their dominion over lands and races unknown to them, in the pre-industrial 18th century used the term 'squatter' to describe a pioneering settler of British Empire in the most distant continents of America, Africa or Australia. Thus, the concept of 'squatters' rights' was used by 19th century (and earlier) British colonialists in order to 'provide entry for settlers to land that was initially ceded to indigenous communities' (Vasudevan 2017, 188). Pre-industrial squatters were invading alien cultures and claiming the land by the force of their war machines – guns. They were colonisers. On the other hand, already in the industrial London of mid-19th century, colonial labourers working in the East End docks started taking abandoned buildings by force – something that was defined later by law as being against the will of the property owner and secured by means of controlling the entrance points. Marginalised global expats moved in great numbers to the London carcass of the British Empire in the 20th century by the time it had become post-industrial.

Those rotting city spaces and social fermentations are also decomposing the extended bodies of post-Internet mutants. The analysis of my performance acts at a squatted, derelict sewage in London engages the environmental context of urban decay in the interrogation of the mutating bodies of the post-Internet performers. I want to suggest that, in the times of global media, squatters have created their own form of a decomposed postcolonial identity, as they come from all over the planet to the previous capital of the global empire – London. Here, they appropriate the waste of urban society by literally going inside it. Going inside means going underground without social gravity, as their occupation is anonymous and their identities non-transparent, and thus virtual. They represent the living process of the decay of urban architecture, which was the past monument of imperialistic glory. (Some of the squatted properties are still the most expensive ones in the world). Squatters thrive without identity like microbial pests, bringing all the issues of postcolonial global entanglement next door. Squatting thus offers an experimental platform for a new mutation of what used to be seen as 'postmodern' lifestyles, spreading as a symbiotic support network beyond the verification systems of humanist identities. The networks of squatting neutralise social waste, reinventing transhuman identities beyond the blurred lines of society. They work as underground tubes of mycelia that form microcanalisation in soil, neutralising neurotoxins with fungal bioremediation. In reinventing trans-identities for the criminalised margin of society, which squatters often represent, they perform as fungi that, with their digestion, facilitate the disposal of chemical weapons (with some fungi being able to consume chemicals such us Indochinese agent orange or sarin Tokyo gas, according to Stamets) as well as of pesticides, herbicides or even radioactivity and other industrial toxins.

Becoming squatters, previous social outcasts become 'socially able' and independent in their life support, yet they still function outside of the social designs of powers that be. They create an extraordinary value of creative subcultures by transforming the initial stigma of social exclusion. Squatters are thus filters for political machinery, just like fungi are biological filters for industrial technology. Squatting can be seen as an example of a remediation process based on spontaneous communication that revitalises exhausted urban environments. In Chapter 3 I will explore this architectural and city-infrastructural embeddedness of fungi media through offering reflections on my own practice of squatting a bio-contaminated sewage (Chronic Illness 2023) – and on the performative engagement with its microbial entities within that space.

CHAPTER 3

The Dungeons of Polymorphous Pan

Entering the Mutating Space

'Chronic Illness' is the organising concept of my performance art practice, which seeks engagement with the nonhuman life of fungoids. In this chapter I critically reflect upon my Chronic Illness activities with a view to preparing the ground for outlining the performance of alternative sexualities through all sorts of bodily mutations, on- and offline. 'Chronic Illness' doesn't reference any specific medical condition but rather introduces a variety of 'trans-corporeal' (Alaimo 2010) approaches to the human body. Trans-corporeal approaches debunk the separation of bodies from their environment, instead defining bodies as momenta of environmental processes. The notion of the Chronic Illness conceptualises bodies that are not complete or harmoniously static; they are chimerical, unevenly distributed, vulnerably porous and involved in dynamic transformations of unknown intensities. 'Chronic Illness' emphasises the penetration of human bodies by microbial agencies and links them in a critical manner to the fungoid environment. We could say this notion prioritises the environmental understanding of bodies by exposing their constant manipulation by, and disintegration into, the moving compounds of nonhuman entities (microbes, fungi). 'Chronic Illness' thus overcomes the limitations of defining human bodies as proportionally composed individual entities, apparently independent from the randomness of live environments. In my conceptualisation of the Chronic Illness I follow the imaginative ideas of writer and actor Antonin Artaud, who attacked societal systems of bodily repression as 'conspiracies' of the healthy against the ill. Artaud challenged the oppressive hierarchies of population control behind the ideologies of 'health' by exploring trans-corporeal vectors of human bodies. For me, the Chronic Illness is not an acute, superficial issue but rather a manifestation of a deep and ongoing conflict within bodies. It never completely goes away but reappears in waves, cyclically performing organic destabilisations and mutations of human bodies via their co-mingling with microbes and fungoids.

The subject of my research is the microbial activity unfolding in the performance space of the Dungeons of Polymorphous Pan, which I've been squatting for over eight years at the time of writing (2015-2023). Over one hundred human body acts have happened there, accompanied by over two thousand participants who have attended the twenty Chronic Illness (of Mysterious Origin) events (Chronic Illness 2023), and who have been part of the ongoing process of communication, via fungi media, of and with the severely bioactive environment. The diversity of fungi, slime moulds and other microbial species has been manifesting itself in the dynamic relations to the multiple contaminations of the space by the human performers' bodies, together with plant and animal bodies, and to the synthetic remains that those bodies have introduced into the space. Moreover, the vital conditions for life in the Dungeons have been provided by the invasive liquids causing humidity, leaks and floods. Those leaks are related to the ground waters affected by the fluctuating weather, filtered through the underground rivers connected to the piping system, as well as the sewage infrastructure's malfunctions and the porous walls of the rotten architecture, in complicity with the perspiration of the human bodies descending into the space.

The name the *Polymorphous Pan*, which was given to the basement 'dungeons' of my squat during the first year of its occupation in 2015, projects intense mutability as the fundamental condition of this space. The space has been occupied and engaged by myself and other human performers, as a laboratory to conduct performative experiments with anonymous substances of fungoid actants. I have called the events taking place there *The Chronic Illness (of Mysterious Origin)* to emphasise the severity of the invasive bodily media which I have started to examine in there. The raw actuality of the dungeons under London's Holloway has served as my living environment for over eight years (my living space is the threshold of the Dungeons of Polymorphous

Pan and the trap door under my bed is the only passage into the space), providing bare conditions for my biological survival. On my arrival, I encountered a space of ambiguous contamination, visibly (and olfactorily) infested with many life entities. Those entities offered an elusive company in conceiving narratives of unknown or alien life forms, carrying imaginary illnesses that recall the mirage of infamous London Black Death bacillus and eventually speculating about psycho-somatic disturbances caused by the lockdown of bodies during the Covid pandemic (Chronic Illness 2023). The mysterious microbial entities have been hiding and irregularly reemerging in unexpected new shapes. From the first moment, I knew that I couldn't observe the entirety of the behaviour of the life forms present in the dungeons, as the pace of life of fungi and other microbes greatly exceeds humans' perceptive capabilities. Nevertheless, my aim has been to make fungoid entities emerge as the living medium for my human understanding by performing with them, and make them perform through acts of human performers. Obsessively, I've been reinventing the fungi media of the mysterious mould embedded at the Dungeons of Polymorphous Pan, developing it as my dirty fetish, or rather what Bruno Latour calls *factish* (Latour 1999). In his science and technology studies work, Latour offers a concept of the experiment that constructs the subject (here, fungoids) through the experimental conditions of this subject's performance, when at the same time the subject (the fungoids) can come to existence only through the experimental performance. In the context of Latour's theory, my fetishisation of microbes and fungi is actually a way of calling them into existence.

In order to introduce fungoids at the Dungeons, I begin by looking at the so-called 'microbe effect', as described by Peters (Peters 2015, 111). The term 'microbe' means 'small life' and designates organisms that are invisible to the human eye. Microbes were discovered over three centuries ago, thanks to advancements in the optical technology of the microscope. Its inventor, Robert Hooke, reported the discovery of microorganisms in 1665, by depicting the microfungus Mucor [fig. 6] in his book *Micrographia* (Hooke 1665). It was published in London during a major outbreak of bubonic plague (the Great Plague of 1665 terminated by the Great Fire of London of 1666), which had also been spread by microbes, but of a different type. The discovery brought to public attention myriads of life forms that were otherwise not perceivable by humans. I applied an artistic method of bodily performance to interrogate fungoids further.

My performative challenge to fungi media in the dungeons of my squat can be compared to Latour's analysis of Pasteur's examination of yeast as the main agent of fermentation at the French biologist's laboratory. Latour points to the creation of yeast ontology by Pasteur from the original anonymous substance, which was vague, grey, irregular and amorphous. He summarises the initial examination of yeast's qualities as follows: 'It would be hard for something to have less

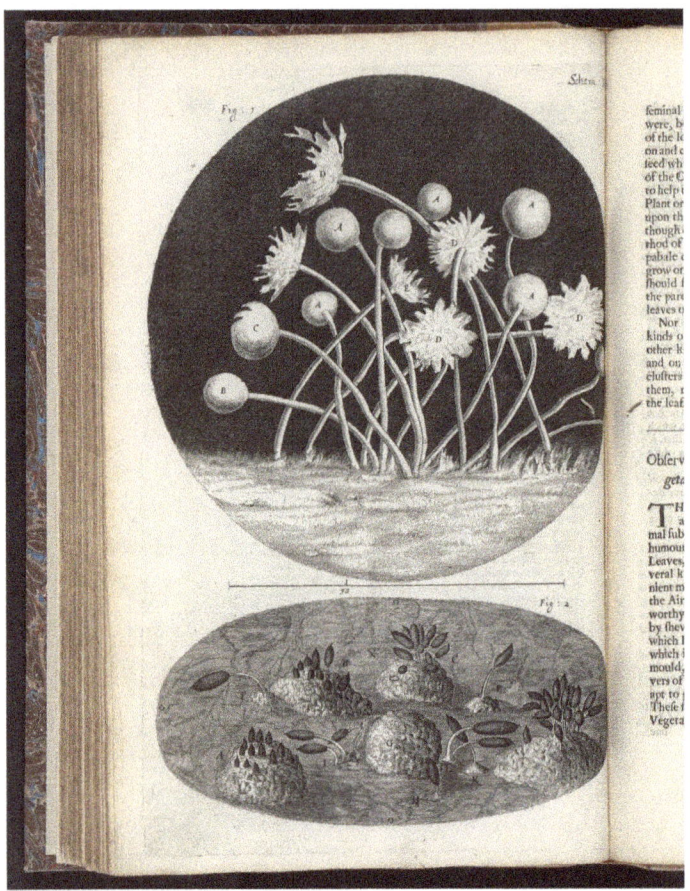

Fig. 6. Robert Hooke, 1665. Scan of the original print of microfungus Mucor hand drawing from *Micrographia* based on observations via handmade microscope (Public Domain).

existence than that. It is not an object, but a cloud of perceptives, not yet the predicates of coherent substance' (Latour 1999, 118). Originating from such a blurry phantom of existence, Pasteur creates his fermenting mould by making it perform certain qualities in response to his laboratory manipulations. The exemplary microbe actually comes into existence as a performer, since 'we do not know what *it is*, but we know what *it does* from the trial, conducted in the lab. A series of performances *precedes* the definition of the competence that will later be made the sole course of these very performances' (Latour 1999, 119). In a similar manner, my curatorial directions of the Chronic Illness art events, and then the acts of the mutant body performers during the events, make fungoids in the basement perform for us and become with us. Pasteur's yeast came into existence as something that could be sprinkled, that triggered fermentation, that rendered a liquid turbid, that made the chalk disappear, that formed a deposit, that penetrated gas, that formed crystals and that became viscous – all in response to the conditions of the laboratory manipulated by Pasteur himself.

Thinking along similar lines, I shall try to define the microbial performance entities in the Dungeons of Polymorphous Pan by provoking their behaviour in response to the conditions of the Chronic Illness events. Bringing out the behaviour of nonhuman living beings through events manipulated by humans, I have to recognise microbes as the actual actors of the Chronic Illness performance art, also understood in analogy to scientific experiments described by Latour: 'there is no other way to define an actor but through its action, and there is no other way to define an action but by asking what other actors are modified, transformed, perturbed or created by the character that is the focus of attention'

(Latour 1999, 122). Yeast as Pasteur's actor emerged in his text only as a performative response to the precise experimental conditions of Pasteur's laboratory. Yet, as Latour points out, Pasteur's text will be authorised mainly by yeast, 'the real behaviour of which can then be said to *underwrite* the entire text' (132). In this sense the intense realness of microbes constitutes the essence of all laboratory manipulations and even makes the science of Pasteur an event in microbes' life (rather than microbes being an event in Pasteur's experimentation). That's why Latour proposes that Pasteur 'happened' (146) to fermenting microbes. In the same vein, I would like to propose that the human performances during the Chronic Illness happened to the microbes occupying the Dungeons of Polymorphous Pan.

My squatted Dungeons are named after the mythological trickster creature Pan Polymorphous. Pan was one of the bestial characters associated with the cult of Dionysus, who allegedly indulged in polymorphic selves whence 'after seeing his image in the mirror went in search of himself everywhere, and considering himself to be plural, developed multiple personalities, and so was ripped apart' (Reed 2006). Following the initial usage of the space as a private venue for 'shibari' – the Japanese practice of body restraint with ropes – the Dungeons were turned into a mould-inspired performance art venue. Their name defined a subterranean realm of corporeal transhumanity associated with the playful bestiality of zoophile god Pan. The bestiality of Pan is not adopted in the Dungeons as a literal sexualisation of animals, but rather as a metaphorical figure of openness towards intimate encounters with nonhuman life. The polymorphous characteristic of the space references the multidirectional perversity and the diverse exploratory forms of bodily trans-identities, described by psychoanalysis as the prime stage of children's eroticism, preceding any fixed objects of desire. In the 'Polymorphous-Perverse Disposition' section of his second essay from *Three Contributions to the Theory of Sex* (aka *Three Essays on the Theory of Sexuality*), Sigmund Freud states that even under the slightest, random influence a 'child may become polymorphous-perverse and may be misled into all sorts of transgressions. This goes to show that it carries along the adaptation for them in its disposition' (Freud 1920). In a psychoanalytic view, children become polymorphous effortlessly, manifesting a 'uniform disposition for all perversions' (Freud 1920). The environmental dispersion of sexuality into the multiple spatial directions of life, the amorphous distribution of the sexual energy that transgresses the human bodily shape, became a figure of polymorphous decomposition experience in the Dungeons. The living space functions as a sewage-ritualistic process of microbial fertility, decomposing organic tissues that human performers bring into it. Here, the shibari practice offers a figuration of the restraint submission of human bodies to the biocontamination of dark waters. Power-play with fungi forces humans into vegetative behaviour and invites the penetration of all skin pores by slimy nanotubes. Polymorphy describes here formally the experimental character of the performance space, where theatrics meet the dynamics of biomedia mutation. Meaning literally 'a multiplicity of forms', the polymorphy of my dungeons invites in particular the performances of elusive biomorphs of fungi and other microbes. Polymorphy also describes the performance environment in terms of its technological possibilities.

In his book *Bodies in Technology* (Ihde 2002), Don Ihde contextualises the term *polymorphy* in the perspective of the phenomenology of bodily mediation, explaining that the intentionality of bodily actions goes beyond the body's limits defined by skin. A 'body experience is one that is not simply coextensive with a body outline or with one's skin. … One's skin is at best polymorphically ambiguous, and, even without material extension, the sense of the here-body exceeds its physical bounds' (Ihde 2002, 6). For Ihde, polymorphy is an inevitable element of human bodily experience. It is at the same time an essential characteristic of transhuman technological embodiments. He proposes that 'Imagining, now technologically embodied, makes polymorphy – particularly of visual shaping – a forefront phenomena' (12). Ihde defines polymorphy in a twofold manner: as 'computer effects that make presumed real entities hyperreal' and as 'the already unreal morphings that either show realistic-looking oddities such as the parasitic alien animals in *Aliens,* or abstract, vaporous … forms, such as the high-speed travel morphing in science-fiction' (12). This double effect of media polymorphy corresponds to the supposed irony of 21st century fantasy simulations, such as computer games that become increasingly 'realistic', and hi-tech instrumentations, applied to the 'realism' of scientific research such as media diagnoses, weather patterns, geology or the mapping of the cosmos, which are apparently ruled by 'something of an inverse proportion law at play – the better the data/image, the more constructed it has been' (Ihde 2002, 136). Once again, Ihde's polymorphy brings us back to Latour's mutual performance of humans and nonhumans. Respectively, the curatorial concept for my performance space is based on the conviction that to understand humans and nonhumans, be they microbes or media or, indeed, fungi media, we must see their interplay in actional situations. This playful complicity with fungoids in the space of polymorphous shape-shifting invites performers and participants to enact their chronic illness.

The Body as a Performance

In an attempt to theorise the mutant performance in the Dungeons of Polymorphous Pan, I would like to reference the presentation of the nonhuman body envisaged by Karen Barad in her article 'Invertebrate Visions: Diffractions of the Brittlestar' (Barad 2014). In the article Barad positions the body of an animal as a discursive practice enacted by means of its performance. 'The importance of the body as a performance, rather than a thing, can hardly be overemphasized' (Barad 2014, 228), she reminds us, while offering a description of the brittlestar's movements in terms of worldmaking. Barad claims that 'practices by which it differentiates between "itself" and the "environment", by which it makes sense of its world – are materiality enacted. Its bodily structure is a material agent in what it sees/knows' (Barad 2014, 227). In this narrative, the performance of the body becomes a process of direct knowledge making. 'Knowledge making is not a mediated activity. ... Knowing is a direct material engagement' (232), she concludes. In this account, media are understood as a direct materiality of life, which is always being performed.

This dynamic quest to enact the human's involvement with nonhuman bodies is the shared motif of all the articles included alongside Barad's in *Multispecies Salon*, a book accompanying a series of bioart performance events in the US (Santa Cruz 2006, San Francisco 2008, New Orleans 2010, New York 2011). The artist-philosophers involved speculate about bioactive media, with a view to finding performative engagement with nonhuman entities of life. In 'R.A.W. Assmilk Soap', coming from her inter-species experience, Karen Bolender expresses a frustrating 'desire to let the wordless interweaving of bodies in time somehow be the act' (Bolender 2014, 72). This act is supposed to offer an insight into the lived world via the vehicles of the bodily performances of nonhumans, which enact 'the quieter, embodied wisdom of the other ones, ... in flesh and fur and mud, beyond all the names and distinctions' (Bolender 2014, 82). Nevertheless, those nonhuman performances actually happen significantly *with* humans, as we are reminded by Eben Kirksey, Brandon Castelloe-Kuehn and Dorion Sagan in their 'Life in the Age of Biotechnology' (2014). I interrogate this notion of performative interdependence between human and nonhuman bodies via my curatorial concept of the Chronic Illness.

Probing ideas on the cross-section of bioart and bodily performance, I was inspired by the Artaudian figure of his totemic disgusting mother (Artaud 1995) [fig. 7] made out of microbial excrement and, as such, being a hybrid proto-humanoid figure emerging from a microbial pile. I adapted that figure to the immersive theatrics of *Chronic Illness 10: Ooze Feed* (Chronic Illness 2023), which was directed around a significant transhuman figure of a monstrous mummy, capable of breeding mutants. The mother figure became the centre point of the scene, dominating the Dungeons and controlling the vectors of movement in the space by giving orders to other mutant-looking performers. She was coated with decaying materials incubating in the Dungeons. Growing from the manhole, her mouldy glands were spurting oat milk, which is a common feed for slimes and some primitive fungi during laboratory tests. My curatorial aim was to withdraw from the human power position of 'controlled experiment conditions' usually assumed by the scientific method in relation to nonhuman life forms. Sucking and spilling slime food, the performers were nourishing their companion microbes. The microbes already transformed the bodies of performers through the partial external digestion of their

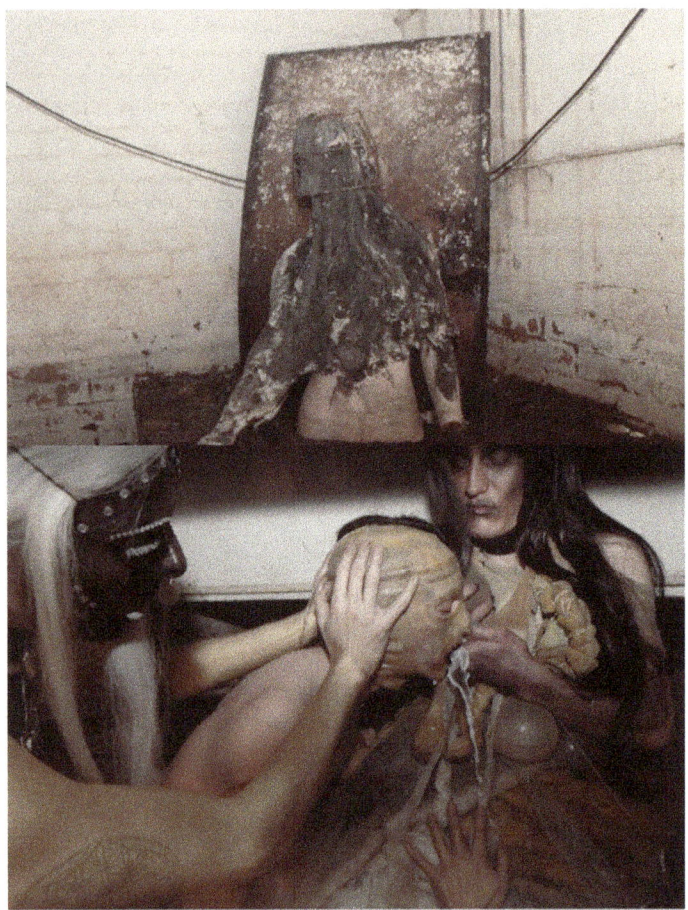

Fig. 7. Yasmine Akim, 2018. *Ooze Feed* directed by
Piotr Bockowski and Alex Avery. Image courtesy of the artist.

costumes and sets, which were an integral part of the organic networks within the live space. Fungoids at the Dungeons were thus being indirectly invented through my curation of the performances there, in an attempt to acknowledge the biomatter as *companions for*, as well as *media of* the human species.

The performances of nonhumans with human bodies assume becomings understood as 'new kinds of relations that emerge from alliances and symbiotic attachments, in contrast to relationships structured by patrilineal descent or filiation' (Kirksey, Costelloe-Kuehn and Sagan 2014, 205). This concept of human-nonhuman becoming postulates horizontal relations between humans and other species, as opposed to the hierarchical concept of human domination over nature. Heather Paxons taps into this idea with her project of *microbiopolitics*, which is a self-proclaimed 'post-Pausterian' manifesto premised on approaching microbes beyond the ideologies of hygiene and antiseptics, with an aim 'to embrace mud and bacteria as potential friends and allies' (Paxons 2014, 116). Similarly, when inviting many human performers to the Dungeons of Polymorphous Pan, I always considered all of the human acts in relation to the life of the mysterious microbial entities in the space, wishing to account for them too [fig. 8]. This approach is echoed in the words of another author included in *Multispecies Salon*, Miriam Simun, who says: 'Never think you know all of the species involved' and 'never think you speak for all of yourself' (Simun 2014, 140). In order to give an account of my involvement in the microbial performance in the Dungeons of Polymorphous Pan, I want to contextualise the space in the organic relations with the metropolitan infrastructure of London, the networks of

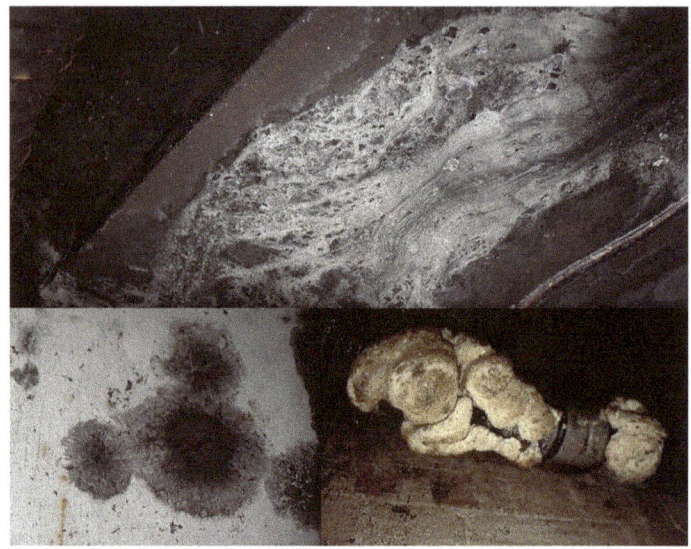

Fig. 8. Piotr Bockowski, 2017. Fungoid life at the Dungeons of Polymorphous Pan.

squatting and the organic media of the Holloway area. They all constitute mutations of the Chronic Illness bodily performances.

Squatting Urban Decay After the Internet

To present the space of the Dungeons of Polymorphous Pan, I shall focus in the further part of this chapter on the situated knowledge I have acquired as a squatter in London, and on the performativity of squatting in relation to fungi media, embodied through the performance art events I have curated. Since 2009 I have been inhabiting abandoned buildings and turning them into performance spaces. The Internet has always been my scaffolding for orchestrating squatting – from using Google Street Maps (and Satellite View) to find locations and possible entry points, through to verifying properties via online real estate listings as well as governmental databases, linking with travellers' websites and anarchist support circuits for urban nomads, as well as promoting events for underground, D.I.Y. and queer art peers on social media. The involvement of social media in my squatting practice pulls those who connect to my squatted spaces into performative situations that Judith Butler would describe in terms of transgressing the body towards the excremental filth of 'Others' (Butler 1990, 170). Performers and participants in the Chronic Illness events step beyond the computer screens to perform the corporeal in a gestural and desirous dimension of my sewage theatrics that produce the meaning 'on the surface of the body' (Butler 1990, 173). I see it as an action of becoming through a micropolitics that challenges the technosystem of social control (also attached to social media such as Facebook and Tumblr, which I use to promote the Chronic Illness), inviting Internet users to 'the dangers that permeable bodily boundaries present to the social order as such' (Butler 1990, 168).

Moving beyond sterile computer simulations, Internet users enter the space of the Chronic Illness, where they rediscover the permeability of their bodies, which are now open for penetration by, and transformations via, fungoid nonhumans. Since its early days, including the pre-Internet era, the whole squatting project has remained physiological in its core challenges, involving the physical trespassing of the architectural space, enforcing the guerrilla practices of taking control over the property and establishing the continuity of occupation within the group resistance towards institutional and other legal pressures, as well as dealing with incidents of raw violence. Finally, the performance artists and peers that find out about the squatted spaces, and that join them as a consequence of following the communications I send out, are eventually confronted with my decaying hideout that exposes their bodies to an experience that transcends the mediation of communication technologies. Through this, I have established a testing ground for my notion of fungi media, which is enacted in this encounter of post-Internet human bodies of the performers with the nonhuman life entities of the rotten inner spaces of the city. My squatting opens up a theatre of an approach to live matter that Jane Bennett defines as a 'playful element' (Bennett 2010, 15). She suggests a strategy of a performative gesture of the human who courageously speculates about the nonhuman, while being aware of not knowing its other but performing with it nevertheless.

The Dungeons of Polymorphous Pan embody fungi media in two ways. They are a performance art space that exercises the notions of post-Internet art (Kholeif 2014), understood as various artistic practices informed by phenomena related to media spaces and communication technologies, but extending them to a physical space and embodying those phenomena in performance art. In this sense the practice of the actual bodies of the performers extends the notions performed by them as Internet users. Here, the strategies for mutation and techno-decomposition meet the corporeal materiality of Internet users. Thus, the fungus presented in the space enables a return of the mediated body to its base materiality. In a way, the fungal performance events assume a form of 'biotic games', which are video games that involve nonhuman agents like microbes that play with humans and computers. My performance practice involves an element of biotic hybridity, as human performers act out with microbes and define themselves through that relation. Online videos from the events mediate human entanglement with microbes. Also, as a special container for the performances, the Dungeons are themselves a figure of fungi media. Embedded in the messy underground of the city infrastructure, contaminated by waste, they encapsulate a bioactive sphere of mould, forming a fungal chamber with the living history of urban stratification in London. My exploration of that special plane of fungi media will start here with some speculations about the dark metaphysics of soil media, the fungal excrement.

The location of the Dungeons of Polymorphous Pan is Holloway, a muddy area in north London. Originally north *of* London, the area was called 'Hollow Way' in the Middle Ages, with reference to the sunk or sloughy highway going through it. 'The "hollow way" was ... "notoriously miry and deep"' (Weinreb 1983, 399), according to the earliest records, a quality that has been internalised by the Dungeons nowadays. Filled with muddy fungoid slime, the Dungeons create a unique dynamic with their excretion. In understanding their materiality, I am inspired by the speculations about the amorphic life processes of microbe matter in the deep space of the Earth outlined in the *blobology* narratives of philosopher Reza Negarestani, who describes the Blob as a 'lubricant of Telluric Lube, upon which everything moves forward, spreading smoothly and inevitably' (Negarestani 2008, 26). In *Cyclonopedia*, Negarestani experiments with different forms of narrating a philosophical fiction. He focuses on the microbial substances dwelling under the surface of the planet whose existence can be traced back to the beginnings of life, and which have been influencing or 'lubricating' the human cultures from the 'telluric' underground, all the way to the civilisations of high technology and media communications all over the surface of our planet. This 21st century speculative philosophy links back to the classic of Soviet SF literature by the Strugatsky brothers. In their influential *Roadside Picnic* they play with an idea of a 'Zone', a mysterious area influenced by alien visitation that literarily breeds unimaginable new technologies. Parallel to some actual reports (Sharp and Graham 2015, 31) on American TV about fungal epidemics supposedly being alien invasions, there was an obscure fungal liveliness to the 'post-visitation' Zone, as:

> It reeked of everything, of lousy fungus that was growing on the Zone, drinking on the Zone, eating, exploiting and growing fat on the Zone and that didn't give a damn about any of it,

> especially about what would happen later, when it had eaten its full and gotten power, and when everything that was once in the Zone was outside the Zone. (Strugatsky 2007, 68)

The transgressive nonhuman performance space of the Zone was filled with the dump expanse of slime. The technological development of humans in the Strugatskys' narrative originates from the risky explorations of the fungus-infested space. Like in the Strugatskys' novel, in Negarestani's philosophy technological civilisation is also powered by the dark vitalism of microbial entities. Negarestani's blobology designates oil as a specific element that animates the ideologies of the deserts of the Middle East, which he is writing about. There is no oil in Holloway, but the fungal discharge plays a similarly animating role for the performers who come to the Dungeons from the outside. The discharge serves as a lubricant for the actions performed in the space, as the all-encompassing decay aesthetic is the primal inspiration and the constant environmental context for the interventions of the performers. Moreover, the regular flooding of the Dungeons, related to the deterioration of the sewage piping in Holloway, gives the space an intense sticky stench quality that changes over time, enabling a palette of sensory repulsions. These repulsions constitute a barrier of social transgression, as the disgusting smell and touch challenge various social norms and taboos that repress the creeping sensorium of decay processes.

The discovery of the blob of semi-life in the guts of the Earth and the recognition of it as an anonymous agency behind human cultures drives Negarestani to postulate the deconstruction of the symbolic systems and to challenge the integrity of identities that are constructed on their basis as well as of the accompanying traditional values. Interestingly, that exegesis is enacted by Negarestani in the chat room of an imaginary website in the book, which describes the Internet as the most 'natural place' to negotiate the disgusting elusiveness of the abject blob. Similarly, in their attempt to overcome their repulsion towards the blob, the performers at the Dungeons find company in the mysterious 'primal interstellar bacterial colonies existing in the bowels of the Earth' (Negarestani 2008, 26). The frequently invading floods of drainage, sewage and ground waters destroy the many surreal forms of slime moulds and fungi that appear in the Dungeons sometimes only for one night, almost unnoticed. The floods also create a nourishing lubrication for the new forms that breed, after the washed-out ones disappear. The microbial corpse juice serves as a slimy medium for the performance acts that take place in the Dungeons.

I squatted the space of the Dungeons in the early days of my research into fungi media in 2015. Thus, the two projects have been developing in parallel, with the Dungeons serving as a testing ground, or laboratory, for exploring notions of post-Internet performativity conceptualised in terms of fungi media research. By post-Internet (Kholeif 2014) I mean the forms of activity of Internet users taken beyond the Internet, at the same time extending the experience of Internet life. As Sarah Kember and Joanna Zylinska point out, 'events and actions, including those performed on our own and others' bodies, are literally informed and ontologically choreographed by images' (Kember and Zylinska 2012, 135) – which are in turn produced by means of communication media. Performance acts in the Dungeons invite communication with the fungoids inhabiting the space by reenacting the behavioural patterns developed online. I represent a polymorphous fungus on social media (using an avatar called 'Neo Fung' & @chronicillness_sewage), which sends out invitations to the Dungeons' events, together with calls for various immersive participants, carrying the virtual spore of the fungi from the squatted sewage. This involvement of technological 'choreography' in life processes is emphasised through the curation of the Chronic Illness events. Performance acts taking place at the Dungeons can be perceived in this vein as embodiments of the possibilities of mutation on the part of the mysterious fungoid entities inhabiting the space, and of post-Internet body artists, performing together with the fungoids.

The Trans-Corporeality of the Chronic Illness

The Dungeons are amplified with electric sound systems and social media (Facebook, Instagram, Vimeo, Tumblr), attracting visitors to join in the collective acts of the 'Chronic Illness of Mysterious Origin' ('Chronic Illness' in short) nights, which constitute temporary immersive environments for the bodily extensions of Internet life. The name *Chronic Illness* evokes a networked understanding of the event participants' bodies, fused with the dynamics of their environment. In her book *Bodily Natures* Stacy Alaimo proposes the term 'trans-corporeal' to name the above approach, exploring the notion that the environment 'runs through us in endless waves' (Alaimo 2010, 11). Apart from its common negative connotation as a threat to life, a chronic illness is inherently fused with the microbial dynamics encompassing the body as well as acting within it. A chronically ill body is in the process of becoming with and through the microbes dispersed through it. Bodies and environs are thus continuous with each other. With a chronic illness in mind, considering diverse transmutations of various materialities into biobodies, via metabolism as well as technologies such as farming or pharma, Alaimo postulates not only a high regard for dirt as a source of life, but also a certain kinship with it. Human flesh is a relative of dirt, according to her.

Analysing media around environmental illnesses, involving malicious microbial bio-agency called 'xenobiotics' (Alaimo 2010, 129), Alaimo shows how chronic illnesses are caused by technological manipulations of the environment and their subsequent impact on bodies. Bouncing off Karen Barad's concept of 'intra-action' (Barad 2007, 170), Alaimo defines bodies through their relations within the environment, which are also technological. At the same time, bodies are defined by Alaimo via an immense impact the environment has on them. She twists the medical understanding of illnesses as unwanted anomalies to proclaim that, as the 'freaks' become more numerous, 'they are no longer anomalies, but a new and viable species' (Alaimo 2010, 139). A critical amassment of freaks turns their chronic illness into a vehicle from the 'material sense of deviation', and towards an 'ideal to openness to unexpected change' (Alaimo 2010, 139). I embrace this 'trans-corporeal' turn in my philosophical curation of the Chronic Illness events, during which dirt performs as art and microbes are considered co-authors of the acts.

My embodied exploration of trans-corporeality has resulted in a performance act called *Synthetic Organs* [fig. 3]. Originating from my obsessive gestures of mapping the Dungeons space as an extension of my own bodily agency, I choreographed my movements around a monstrous wound sculpted into the squat's wall. The fleshy membrane of the wound was made out of the same synthetic material as the body deformities attached to me, mixed with the dirt from the space. My gestures in the performance act were an attempt to relate the changing body shape to the environmental membrane of the wall-wound, thus establishing a trans-corporeal dynamic of the Chronic Illness. In the middle of the wound a piece of animal gut had been hidden, persevered by androgynous performer Alexander Dodge-Huber as a figuration of his hospitalisations in psychiatric units. I had kept the gut planted in the soil at the rear end of the Dungeons as a germinating reminder of the sickly superiority of his sensitivity over the crude societal ideas of 'health'. Exotic plants used to grow next to the main electric fuse of the space, where I noticed the slime mould lurking in the shadows.

My movements effectively aligned the anatomy of the buildings with the imaginary architecture performed by my monstrous body. Richard Crow mixed my live body sounds with recordings of inner organs sounds made for medical purposes and with archival recordings from the psychoanalytical therapy of Freud's patient Schreber. Schreber had been obsessed with the phantom movements of his inner organs, claiming that they were shifting inside his body or even disappearing and reappearing, while changing their functions. As Crow explains, 'I've read Freud's notes on Schreber: he had delusions that weren't sexual, and these affected him more severely than his gender dysphoria. Schreber believed that his internal organs were vanishing and reappearing' (Richard Crow in Internet chat with Piotr Bockowski, London, 28.10.2016 19:09). I developed my *Synthetic Organs* act for *Chronic Illness of Mysterious Origin 4* [fig. 9] (Chronic Illness 2023) by playing with the paranoid notion of a whimsical organ dynamic, where organs functioned as objects of traumatic projections.

The choreography of *Synthetic Organs* was greatly inspired by the study of the neurotic body by Tatsumi Hijikata, who was arguably the first and most radical executor of Artaud's vision in his development of a conceptual dance resembling an infectious disease. In order to convey the fleshy quality of media I allude here to the theory of dance performance as an exquisite example

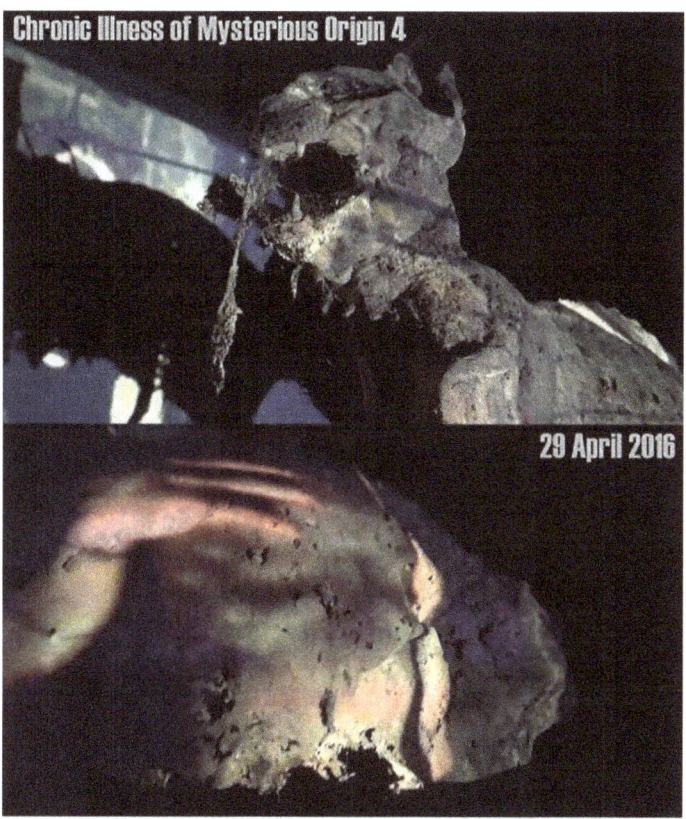

Fig. 9. Piotr Bockowski 2016. Promotional image for the *Chronic Illness of Mysterious Origin 4* event, featuring documentation of *Holobiont*.

of the body's psychopathology. Against the notions of the 'dematerialisation' of media and 'mind singularity', or detached ideas of artificial intelligence (Kurzweil 2013), I understand media by noticing and emphasising how technology violates the body in a non-obvious way, often through the pleasure drive. Stephen Barber sums up this idea in his book on Hijikata's Tokyo project of the dance of darkness called *butoh*: 'Artaud had called for the human body to be urgently anatomised and reconstructed on an autopsy table; ... true dance, in an organ-less, "wrong-way-round" frenzy of gesture, resonant of the delirious dancehalls' (Barber 2006, 29). The surrealist urge to anatomise the human body and reshape it as no-longer-human is being evoked here. Looking at the human body through the subtleties of the inner connectivity of communication technologies, there is a chance to perceive the common processes of the body, or its integral functions and features, as alien if not monstrous forms of excess, revealing the bestiality of organs and the sheer raging absurdity of the members' shapes. The randomness of its proportions is accompanied by an obscene activity of gland secretions, which Artaud insistently described in his poetry as one of the primal processes of abjection, preceding any thought or meaning of organic functions. This dance of the body against itself, an unsettling dance within the body, transgresses the separation between organs and their functionality as a vital context for bodily performance. It also entails a discovery of a nonhuman disease animating the human body against human attempts to conceal that alien agency with the numbing concepts of health and wellbeing.

In the Schreber case, Freud analysed a bodily landscape of a psychosomatic illness, disturbed in its integrity, which consists of 'softening of the brain', hyperaesthesia and hypochondria. This is what Freud wrote about Schreber: 'in association with coenaesthetic disturbances, [visual and auditory delusions] governed all his feelings and thoughts; he held himself to be dead and rotting, suffering from the plague, imagined that all manner of dreadful manipulations were being carried out on his body' (Freud 2002, 6). This rotting experience of the body was performed through imaginary dreadful manipulations on the body transgressed into a fantasy plague within. Schreber would claim that his inner organs were shifting, changing places within the body, changing their shape or function as well disappearing and reappearing as completely new body parts. Those still avant-garde psychoanalytical manipulations clearly evoke the much more contemporary and recent manipulation of visual media, e.g., the 3D art of Jesse Kanda, involving cancerous, bloated and twisted deformities extending bodies into pirouetting digital post-organic landscapes.

For the *Synthetic Organs* project, Crow mixed Schreber's voice, sourced from Internet archives, with my own live screams, hisses, cries, laughs, whispers and deranged lullabies, all literally directed towards my artificial body parts during the act. The organs were loosely attached around my torso, so I could move them around thus changing their location, along with my changing expression towards them. In this way, *Synthetic Organs* visually explored the idea of body-therapy that links psychopathology with physiological deformities. The recognition of the monstrous glands through touch and scream created a new bodily identity for the performer as well as expressing an imaginary trauma. During the performance the synthetic organs, attached to the body of the performer, were discharged as miscarried brood, retarded bastard problem-children. I attempted to lure my decomposing body parts into some sort of complicity with my overall bodily dynamic, relating to them with aggressive rage and desperate cries of perverted cannibalism, or with the semi-erotic tenderness of breastfeeding the parasite, or maybe even by feeding my sacrificed body to an alien ancestor. Taking all those possibilities into consideration, the synthetic organs also enacted my aborted bastard children, scientifically curious excrements, disgusting food, infected genitals, overgrown glands swollen with discharge, beloved cancerous accelerations of the body. Moreover, they attracted me to obsessive acts of fingering an excessive wound the size of my head, opening a crack in a wall of the plant solution container.

Through all this, *Synthetic Organs* became a performance of transhuman bodily entanglements. It explored the relations within the body though diverse material interventions, thus shifting the meaning of the body as such. In Barad's terms (Barad 2003), performativity describes primary epistemological involvement in the world of phenomena. Language cannot function as a representational abstraction separated from the world, because it is always already a material rearrangement *of* the world. The world as phenomena is a relational tangle that ontologically precedes the relata, such as the world of things or thoughts. The performativity of discourses

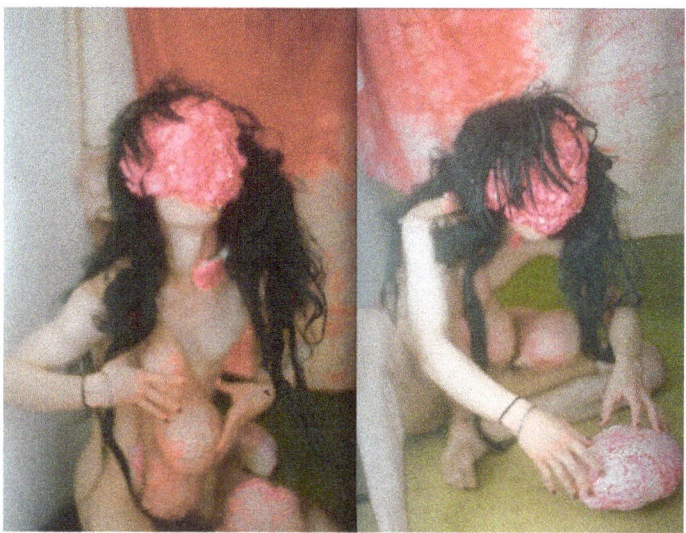

Fig. 10. HTV, 2017. Photography of the *Synthetic Organs* act by Piotr Bockowski.

is essential in creating those and any other distinctions within the world of phenomena. Categories of human or nonhuman are local and temporary possibilities, performed as intra-actions that are always secondary to the relational tangles of phenomena, which they emerge from. Intra-actions are actions producing local meanings by means of *cuts* within the wholeness of phenomena. Thus, performativity stands for the becoming of the human – and of the nonhuman. According to Barad's metaphysics of performativity, the world or nature is a historically limited inner distinction within the phenomenal entanglement. This *halfway meeting* between the performativity of discourse and phenomenal matter, with its own histories, informs Barad's methodology of *agential realism*, which is employed by the acts of *being-doing* of the performers' indeterminate body mutations in the Dungeons.

Following Barad's methodology, Alaimo reminds us again that agency is unrelated to human subjectivity and that performance of material agencies is a more valid way of making sense of the world than restrictive human mind-supremacist representations of bodies as 'things': 'Dirt demonstrates all agency without agents, a foundational, perpetual becoming that happened without will or intention or delineation' (Alaimo 2010, 145). My curatorial project of the Chronic Illness thus becomes a symptom of posthumanism that emphasises material interrelatedness of all nonhumans with humans as well as machines, all embedded in a 'fleshy matrix of generativity' (Alaimo 2010, 154). At the same time, it is important to remember that the extraordinary ecological role of dirty microbes as decomposers does not lie in their direct usefulness as producers of new life forms. Writing about her 'new vitalism', Claire Colebrook even argues that the vitality of matter does not lie in its creativity but rather in 'inertia and passivity' (Colebrook 2008). According to her, the intensity of life is embedded in the voiding of decomposition, which exposes matter beyond the forms imposed on it.

When developing my Chronic Illness performance events, I chose the aesthetic of bodily deformity and the degeneration of organic matter with an aim to expose those phenomena as particularly advantageous for the generative processes of life. The condition of a chronic illness defines the body of the performers as unbalanced or disturbed, internally conflicted and triggered by unknown environmental conditions. The exploration of the imaginary state of an illness became my performance method, which was paramount to embracing the difficult complexity of living bodies.

The events' participants (drawn, as previously explained, from social media), took the risk in moving beyond the Internet and into my fungoid performance space, where they got involved in my immersive acts. There was no actual illness involved in the events, but the presence of the participating bodies created a communication platform that embodied ideas of disruptive media cultures. Direct involvement with fickle materialities of nonhuman bodies had been conceptualised at the Dungeons against the repressive ideas of 'health', which were considered to be detached from the always uncertain material environments of life. The performance events also tapped into the post-industrial fascination with sickly looks in the fashion and media worlds of recent years. This fascination evokes a time when the wide spread of illnesses in the urban slums of factory workers and the newly emerging semi-nomadic impoverished population of metropolitan areas became a reality in many cities at the end of the 19th century.

The fungal infection of tuberculosis (TB in short), which was breeding in the dumpy overcrowded shelters for the poor, mystified decadent high society, according to Susan Sontag. 'Health becomes banal, even vulgar,' (Sontag 1977, 26) she wrote, as the mysterious deadly illness became associated with a state of higher feelings, since the sufferers of TB were supposed to obtain perceptive faculties much greater than those possessed by the healthy. The paranoid contingency of TB sought sophistication in the aesthetics of decomposition that was consuming the human body. 'Corruption' or 'corrosion' was the old English meaning of the word 'consumption' (Sontag 1977, 10), as opposed to today's notion of 'consumption' in consumerist society. The 'disintegration, febrilization, dematerialization' (Sontag 1977, 13) of TB stood for the liquefaction of the body and was related to the body liquids such as phlegm, mucus, sputum and blood. Many invasive lubrications of that 'wet disease, a disease of humid and dank cities' (Sontag 1977, 15), gave it a perversely moist erotic allure. Romantic literature presented TB as the disease of exquisite passion, apparently originating in the repression of desire (Sontag 1977, 22) as mycomicrobes were infecting the human bodies that were disconnected from their primal drives. The repression of the human's 'original polymorphous perversity', according to Freud, caused an anxious proliferation of 'non-normative' sexual differences. For Sontag, the illness was 'the body's treachery' (Sontag 1977, 40) and in the particular case of TB the prime awakening of the human body was driven by nonhuman natures. The art of the industrial revolution portrayed somnolent belles of tubercular youth and sexy figures of infected courtesans, their attractiveness intensified by the hosting of invasive microbial entities. The industrial decadents imagined TB 'to be an aphrodisiac and to confer extraordinary powers of seduction' (Sontag 1977, 13), at the same time when the gushes of extra energy were in fact the self-destructive signs of internal decomposition. Already then, in the wake of the global industry, the visual transformation of the human body by a fungal infection became the obsessively ambivalent image of new technology.

Fungoid Dwelling in Dark Humidity

The space of the Chronic Illness acts is officially empty, while in reality being occupied by anonymous dwellers. The squatting of the Dungeons of Polymorphous Pan reintroduces bodily porousness to the human-designed compartmentalisation of the London city space, challenging its controlled shapes with the flood of urban migrants taking over the decomposing architecture. The Dungeons, forming an underbelly of an abandoned building, are occupied by a group of Eastern-European city nomads. The space has no *identified* inhabitant, only featuring the vague entity of 'unknown occupiers' (which is the official term used to describe squatters in London). As fungoids, the squatters have no visible identity. Anonymous dwellers of the ruins turned performers of fungi media thus function as decomposing entities of the urban tissue. Alaimo writes that decay 'bacteria build cities within' the human corpses they decompose. Inside the empty shells of urban planning, squatters build dirty slums out of trash, nesting spores of monstrosity that can come across as 'subhuman' or even as an 'illness of society' to the civil authorities.

The squatted 'savage' sewage of the Dungeons channels many narrations around urban natures, buried under the city's infrastructure. It is also a place where I live, read and produce my research into fungi media, typing it on my laptop here and now.

When I first entered the abandoned building in Holloway at the beginning of 2015, I discovered that its basement had been used for the farming of some exotic plants, fed with electric light and microbial solutions, prior to the arrival of my squatters group. Fungi were eating scattered floral tissue in the darkness. Since then, the humidity of the space has been lubricating the surfaces of the Dungeons, rendering them bioactive. The porous old bricks sweat with goo that feeds the diversity of slime moulds, sometimes creating puddles of life or even floods in the squat space. Underground urban floods can be associated with the lost rivers of London that became covered with city infrastructures during the process of 19th-century industrialisation (Barton 1992). The Dungeons are located in the area of the river sources of the Hackney Brook, which used to cross from Holloway through North Hackney to the river Lea in Wick. The river still exists, hidden under the city, apparently merged with the labyrinths of sewage piping. The disappearance of the Hackney Brook was part of the mid-19th century industrial extension of the river Thames, which was badly polluted, into hundreds of miles of the sewage piping system that, at the time, defined London as the biggest metropolitan area on the planet. Even before the arrival of the London

Underground and its grandiose event of excavating tube networks under the ground of London, the monstrous city had been defined by its water pipe system (Weinreb 1983, 924). The sewage was invented as a cleansing infrastructure for the many diseased city rivers that, during the Industrial Revolution, turned into waterways of lethal epidemics. Canalisation was built to filter human waste and channel it towards the industrial slums of east London. I suspect that the nanotubes of mycelium merged almost immediately with this large-tube infrastructure of heavy industry.

At the very end of 2016 the Dungeons witnessed the most severe flooding from the pipes under Holloway Road. The water rose over the knees of the performers, touching our waists. Engaging with this disastrous climate change of the space, I imaged the situation as a reemergence of the repressed river source of the Hackney Brook that was forced into mergence with the Victorian sewage, which ended up cracking after over a century and a half. At the beginning of 2017 I directed *Chronic Illness 8: Ablution* (Chronic Illness 2023) as an ablution ceremony in the sewage waters. Participants were entering the dark space of dirty liquidity and moved on mechanical platforms over the surface of the water, with only scarce traces of light glistening and amorphous piles of trash floating in between the concrete columns. Before entering the Dungeons, the participants had their limbs washed by the performers in a human-size water tank containing slime. All were descending down into a canalisation rite of passage through the bioactive liquid, submerging into its microclimate and carried by platforms moving through the surface of the dark water. The liquidity of the human bodies of the performers and participants became defined by the immersion in the liquid entities of microbes. On the other side of the dark water expanse the platform was delivering participants to a small island of concrete elevation with a tent made out of plant materials. The performance act involved a sensory deprivation of the participants in the dark depths of the Dungeons, beyond the separation of vegetative life forms. The participants were involved in a variety of tactile situations in the darkness – starting with descending down a muddy ladder, then sliding on a moist surface of the moving platforms over the water, pushing against concrete pillars and sensing floating entities all the way into the depths of the space to find warm bodies of the performers lurking in the murk. Later I pumped out the dark water back onto Holloway Road. My curation of *Chronic Illness 8: Ablution* introduced a two-year long period of experiments with immersive theatre animated around the movement of dark water as the medium of fungal life in the Dungeons.

    The creation of London as the world's largest urban complex after the industrial revolution was carried out by means of the repression of the ground waters, which eventually leaked into the Dungeons through the micropores of old bricks. This technological repression, revealed by the Dungeons, presents yet another example supporting the hypothesis that civilisation is being built on geological trauma, understood as the physical suppression of the previous biological infrastructures. The Cybernetic Culture Research Unit (CCRU 2017), which was active at the University of Warwick in the 1990s, researched the phenomenon of 'geotrauma', a term which I have adopted here to help me think about the grounding condition of the Dungeons. The term describes the catastrophes separating the material potencies of the biosphere's body. It relates to the hypothetical trauma of the ancient microbe ancestry. I'm particularly interested in using the concepts of trauma and chronic illness to map my performance space of the Dungeons with the deep understanding and accentuation of the space being a live entity, consisting of organic networks that performers use to communicate. Those fungoid networks dwell in dark humidity under the ground.

Commenting on the symbiogenesis theory of Lynn Margulis, Nick Land (Land 2011, 458) focuses on the traumatic experience of bacteria in the early stages of the development of life on our planet. According to the scenario offered by him, the nucleus of an organised cell, a cell that would later form a prototype unit of multicellular organisms of plants and animals, was created as a result of the mergence of bacteria in reaction to the overfilling of the atmosphere with oxygen excretion. The nucleus cell structure was apparently a form that adapted to oxygen, surviving the extermination of the unknown species of primal bacteria after their exposure to the emerging air atmosphere.

Scientific accuracy is less relevant in Land's traumatic scenario: what is more important is his usage of this story as a reference point for a geo-mythological origin of advanced life. The speculative event of the extermination of primal bacteria serves in Land's narration as a figure of the traumatic experience of microbes that the development of life on Earth originates from. He describes life in environmentally sensitive terms, as a series of traumatic disorders and their chronic conditions. Humans, separated from the prehistoric microbes with the whole time-distance of the evolution of life on Earth, can reconnect with the primal life via media technologies. In that context, media apparatuses can be understood as therapeutic tools for organised life. The opening up of humans to communication with microbes, via transhuman technologies of fungi media, unfolds the layers of the repressed intensities of microbes stratified in the Earth's sediments. The performative space of the Dungeons of Polymorphous Pan can therefore be seen as an attempt to explore the difficult origin of life through media.

According to Land's analysis of 'cosmic repression', our biosphere contains the energy of the Sun internalised inside the planet through the prehistoric layerings of dead biomatter. Robin MacKay follows Land's narrative, pointing out that 'the geologists had already established that the entire surface of the earth and everything that crawls upon it is a living fossil record, a memory bank rigorously laid down over unimaginable aeons and sealed against introspection;

churned and reprocessed through its own material' (Mackay 2012, 16). This perspective envisions the suppression of the molten outer surface of the Earth into its burning iron core as the crucial process in the development of our planet's biosphere. Some proto-life particles had allegedly been trapped deep underground. As CCRU researchers Mackay and Ray Brassier put it, 'What howls for release in eukaryotic cells, carbon molecules, nerve ganglia, and silicon chips, are the thermic waves and currents, deranged particles, ionic strippings and gluttings, that populate the planet's seething core' (Mackay 2012, 40). In the CCRU narration of geotrauma, the experience of repression of the prehistoric microbes formed human bodies by promoting evolutionary emphasis on oxygen dependency. According to the natural philosophy of CCRU, all cultures of human civilisation in some way appear as encrypted messages of the underground layers of the Earth sent to outer space. From this perspective, an individual biological organism seems as old as the biosphere. The biological is defined by Mackay and Brassier as a map of geological time. According to their speculations, current changes to our climate connect humans to the prior evolutionary stages of the microbial forms of life. Human cultures are recognised as compulsive-repetitive symptoms of geotrauma. Those symptoms are being triggered by the conflicted relationship to the energy sources of biology, developed by the first microbes.

Philosophical-fictional narratives of the prehistoric catastrophes of proto-life on Earth developed by authors such as Land, Mackay and Brassier present the biosphere as enacting the dynamics of planetary trauma. In such narratives, the origin of life on Earth got repressed to the very core of the planet, called *C'htell*, 'and every living individual that ever existed is a playback copy, drawn from the recording vaults, trapped in a refrain that sings the glory of Cthell' (Mackay 2012, 19). In his account of Cthell, Mackay presents the individuality of humans as secondary to the microbial entity. Similarly, in my curation of the events in the Dungeons of Polymorphous Pan, I always intend to position the human performers as secondary to the microbial entities that live there and constitute the bioactive space itself. The space serves for me as a laboratory environment to probe the aforementioned geotraumatics with mycelial strategies of performative interventions, infiltrations and infections. I observe the performers as embodying a simulation of a collective fungal entity, embedded in the underworld of the Dungeons, in their acts. According to the CCRU thinkers, the life of humans and most other organisms encapsulates the state of the chronic illness of primal microbes.

The Chronic Illness performance nights provide an opportunity for the dispersed bodies of Internet users to encounter the mysterious mould and project the patterns of their media behaviour onto that alien fungoid entity. Once again, the performing bodies become different mutations, morphed with the poetics of decay liquidity. Recalling, after Woodard, the void energetics of liquid dust and the exuberance of cavities, I see the Dungeons as a space for the media holes of performance entities instead of the wholes of bodily identities. This dark becoming of what Woodard terms *necrotic vitalism* recognises 'thought as a gaseous rot' (Woodard 2012b, 220). He is translating human identities, based on thought, into an ontology of decay. The creeping dynamic of rot folds objective definitions of life and negates the existence of individual species as it undermines distinctions between clear and discrete identities of bio-forms. Woodard exposes rot as the essential circumstance of life and reveals its mediatic character. 'Life itself under certain circumstances becomes articulated as a medium' (Kember and Zylinska 2012, xiii), argue Kember and Zylinska. With this, technology introduces certain openings into the integrity of human identities.

The remaking of the self through the interfaces of communication networks also means becoming multiple – not just multiple selves but also multiple erasures of selves. In this sense, the self of a mediated body becomes a network of the 'lacks of selves', a punctured structure of anti-identities visualised by a dynamic pattern of holes. 'The halo of individuation becomes irreparably poxed. Since wholeness itself is degenerate, since anything as a thing is merely a hole complex, pre-perforated' (Woodard 2012b, 214). The holes mark the wounds of the patients of facial transplant surgery analysed by Kember and Zylinska, opening their bodies to the technologies involved in the reworking of bodily identity. The holes also represent the fragmentary simulations of selves and introduce discontinuities into the networked self. The dynamics of holes encapsulates the process of mediating the body. Media obsession with reuploading the imagery of self-representation can be recognised as a symptom of the 'body dysmorphic disorder', as long as 'there is always a feature of the face or the body that requires "work"' (Kember and Zylinska 2012, 138). This emptying out of the self and the opening to the technological processes of media becoming can also offer a chance of a new relationality, considered after Rosi Braidotti to involve bounding with radical otherness. The latter is understood as 'life's destructive force: all life is a process of breaking down, she [Braidotti] repeats' (Kember and Zylinska 2012, 148). The post-Internet space of the Dungeons offers a unique platform to perform the fractured entities of fungi media bodies.

Due to the almost complete lack of ventilation and the perforation of walls with micro-holes oozing thick liquids, the Dungeons of Polymorphous Pan retain the humid density of a quasi-tropical climate, which is emphasised by the tropical-like wetness and the still air in the space. 'Now cyberpositive diseases are spreading strange tropics to the metropolis' (Land and Plant 1994, 5), argue Nick Land and Sadie Plant when commenting on the new technological nature, which is changing the high-tech cities. They add that 'computer viruses melt icebergs of data down the screens, burning through the bacterial frost' (Land and Plant 1994, 8). Here, post-technological geo-atmospheric effects develop within the concrete chambers under Holloway, with a 'necrovital' aim to elude the techno-control over life through opening urban-tropical environs of the squatted sewage. As Land and Plant speculate, 'strategy tends to come apart in tropics. Even traditional counter-tactics of surveillance and interrogation are becoming obsolete' (Land and Plant 1994, 7). The undoing of the mass-produced techno-designs of life invites new mediations of dispersed corporealities. The urban tropics of my sewage inspire the mutant aesthetics of bodily performance.

The Dungeons embody an industrial-tropical thicket in the clime of its urban geology, pursuing the theatre of contamination and the fetishism of mysterious infections. Performers engage here with 'the decomposed life' of communication technologies through phenomena such as the half-life of detritus or the replication of dusty degraded biomass. In order to embrace the architectural design of the sewage I orchestrated *Chronic Illness 9* as a public urination fetish ritual. The bodies of the performers and participants were locked in the Dungeons for hours, surrounded by flowing sewage water distributed around them by two industrial pipes. My regulative curatorial concept for the plethora of acts, which happened that night, was to stimulate physiologically ritualised urine-passing behaviour of the participants and performers, and orchestrate other acts around that. Everybody was drinking large amounts of green tea in the presence of several shrines dedicated to slime moulds. Enclosed in the dark liquid-mediating body of architecture, humans were repeating the process of channelling liquids through their own bodies.

The performance became essentially a methodical dissolution of the solid definitions of human bodies within fluid connections of the fungal life environment.

My mutant performance events took over a space of the submerged architecture of decay, investigating urban sewage as a form of human dwelling in crisis. The North London suburbs turn into a monstrous fungus formation in the novel *The Drowned World* by J.G. Ballard, which imagines a post-technological transformation of the planet through the awakening of the prehistory of microbial life within human bodies. Ballard describes the landscapes of ancient organisms that overtake the high-tech metropolis of the past and at the same time appear as a reflection of the 'psychic landscapes' of the humans who witness the transformation, which is also an embodiment of 'an ancient memory millions of years old' (Ballard 1997, 74). As the planet witnesses the violent theatre of human technology-induced climate change into an extreme tropical environment, humans witness the mass devolution of life forms and experience a form of evolutionary déjà vu. 'Here we are re-assimilating our biological past' (Ballard 1997, 91), they conclude, as they tap into a recapitulation of their own evolutionary stages via mind-states recalling the deep memories of the primal life forms, imprinted in their bodies. There is a barrier of fungal biomass forming around the submerged London, which embodies hidden neuronic complexes of a London inhabitant. Ballard uses the notion of returning to 'the primeval swamp' (4) not only through the destruction of the urban landscape by natural cataclysm but also by discovering its live existence buried within human bodies. 'Just as psychoanalysis reconstructs the original traumatic situation in order to release the repressed material, so we are now being plunged back into the archaeopsychic past, uncovering the ancient taboos and drives that have been dormant for epochs' (4), writes Ballard. In his narrative, human individuality is decomposed by the return to the 'dark ocean' that is the source of its life and its graveyard. Human transience mediates the extreme power sources of microbes entangled with technology-assisted devolution of the biosphere. In this perspective, explored in my work, media are live material processes that destroy the integrity of human identities together with illusions of natural harmony. They return to haunt the human mind as a constant threat of catastrophic climate change or another natural disaster. In the Ballardian imagination technologies stand for the deep involvement of humans with nature, which is understood as an undetermined performance of dark vitalism.

Urban infrastructures of human dwelling reveal humans' embedding in the obscure life of decomposition when they connect, merge and overwrite the necropolis of catacombs. This archetype of human civilisation's architecture from the tombs of the ancients becomes reworked in Ballard's text into the construction of modernist tower blocks. Connected as they are via electric cables, the tower blocks transform through various designs into a postmodern IT protocol embodied by intelligent architecture, which for Ballard also reveals the psyche of contemporary humans. The datacombs of high-tech global civilisation redefine the human eroticism into deadly transhuman fetishism, as they replace the human object of desire with a technological one, while rendering reproduction obsolete. Ballard defines techno-sex imagination within urban architecture through apparatuses of perverted intimacy (Ballard 1990) or imaginary perversions, asking 'an interesting question – in what way is intercourse per vagina more stimulating than with this ashtray, say, or with the angle between two walls? Sex is now a conceptual act' (Ballard 1990, 61). Human desires are meshed with their technological infrastructures in the form of necro-techno-pornography, as desires become more intensely embodied by the fetishes of apparatuses' cruelty. Car design eroticises the skeleton mutilated in a crash on a flyover junction. Modernist concrete tower blocks of council flats and luxurious real estates implode reality into a hyperbole of the collective nervous system. An intersection of London opens as a living flesh of people who live in the futuristic suburbs of the city, which means that people inhabiting the urban environment are defined by it on the physiological level.

Ballard pictures the human body as part of the city infrastructures, which collapsed into its own sewage. Technology becomes an acceleration of the human characteristics into a surreal overcoming of humanity. The integrity of the human body disperses into an abstraction of technological environments. 'The line between inner and outer landscapes is breaking down. Earthquakes can result from seismic upheavals within the human mind. The whole random universe of the industrial age is breaking down into cryptic fragments' (Burroughs 1990, 3), writes Burroughs, commenting on Ballard. Moreover, Woodard points out that Ballardian visions of urban civilisation's decay revive the deep-time past of primordial life on our planet (Woodard 2013, 145). At the same time, the faculties of the human bodies of Ballard's characters become accelerated and separated by technological fetishisms that replace them.

In McLuhan's biotechnological imagination, media are understood as extended forms of the functions of the human body. Thus, architecture extends the heating system of the organism in the same way that clothes extend the skin. Interestingly, historically clothes production involved the appropriation of plant or animal dead tissue. Since the introduction of industrial wear for the human body, clothes have been made out of chemicals produced with the oil fuel that comes from prehistoric microbes. Cars, in turn, are containers for a portable human body. They encapsulate reality into an internalised form of a control panel, which can relate to the womb or even be sexually charged by a close fit of their interior ergonomics or the bio-design of seats. As vehicles, cars also extend our legs in the narration of McLuhan, as they replace their functions with amplified motor motion. The new environment therefore defines a new body. The core idea of McLuhan is that the human nervous system extends into the environment of electric media. Communication networks perform human cognitive processes and create a new experience of reality by changing proportions between senses involved in perception, reshaping the physiology of the brain and impacting on all other body infrastructures, thus affecting the direction of human becoming. From the perspective of McLuhan, this transformation can be described as a techno-evolution of the human species. The processes of the medial extensions of human bodies define their global expansion by stretching and dispersion at first, but at the same time they incorporate the planet into the human body. Employing McLuhan's concept of extensions (McLuhan 2001), Ballard also connects technology with the primal formations of life that reveal themselves to be animated by human technology and that eventually undo human bodies in visions of post-technological devolution. Mediated human bodies act as bio-cells that eat themselves after the death of their organism, starting the process of rot.

Intelligible Devolution

The notion of mutant performance finds affinities with CCRU's somewhat bizarre geo-speculations. In their interview with Professor D.C. Barker, sound is used as an interrogation tool of the Earth's deep time. Barker recommends to 'fast forward seismology and … hear the earth scream' (Land 2011, 499). The traumatic scream of geology informs the theory of planetary dynamics based on repressed energy in the pre-history of life on Earth, accumulated within the molten magma, which is hidden underneath the surface crust, hosting bio-bodies. According to Barker, the exploration of that deep context for the evolution of life can be done by means of 'convergent waves, without subordination to chronology, history, or linear causation. They proceed by infolding, involution, or implex' (Land 2011, 503). Infolding and involution as directionalities for mediatising life can be recognised as forms of the technological implosion of the human body in the process of the decomposition of fungi media. The body has seemingly reached the limits of its expansion with the acceleration of global economy that threatens humankind with the possibility of extinction as an effect. The imminent folding of technology, due to energy exhaustion or shortage of material resources, offers scenarios of devolution as a possible solution to the crisis of techno-evolution.

The key methodological idea here lies in understanding communication technologies through obscure and negative (in the sense of undoing the body) material processes of decomposition. This approach renders matter intelligible, not in an essentialist way but rather in relation to its behaviour and functional integration. As Negarestani proposed in his lecture for *Symposium: Speculations on Anonymous Materials* in Kassel (Negarestani 2014), human and nonhuman thoughts, and the selves defined by those thoughts, are materials that become apparent only through manipulation or amplification. Negarestani's behaviour principle recognises the intelligence of material systems through their behaviour. All material processes recognised in terms of behaviour can be considered intelligent, a conclusion which transforms all materiality into a living problem. Negarestani proposes the heuristics of approaching problems by means of an intervention of transferring the behaviour of a material form onto a different material form, in order to understand life beyond the objectification of a given substance. I am allowing myself an analogous manoeuvre in my project of fungi media, as I recognise the intelligence aspects of communication technologies by transferring them onto the behaviour of fungi, thus perceiving media as a form of life and life as a form of media. This method of transferring behaviour of life forms between different levels of complexity in living environments is also the key strategy for constructing narratives in Negarestani's *Cyclonopedia*.

One of the forms of material behaviour analysed by Negarestani is the pore pressure of the 'hole complex' (Negarestani 2008, 48), which defines a plane of performative dimension of a space. It can be related to the performance acts under Holloway (the Hollow Way), alongside the variety of microbial activities as well as flooding of the Dungeons [fig. 11]. In this theoretical perspective, the cavities of the Dungeons, with their moisturising activity of ground water micro-leaks and punctured piping, already offer an intelligible narration. They formulate the 'hidden writing' (Negarestani 2008, 60) of plot holes. In contrast to the memory synthesis of linear reasoning that is timeline-based, the plot holes of memory gaps function beyond chronological progression. 'Memory holes introduce gaps, discontinuations tunnels and porous spaces into the chronological sphere of memory, thus making it more prone to time-lapses, abrupt schizophrenic katabases, personality-pulverising blackouts' (68), offers Negarestani. The space of the Dungeons embodies the plot holes of my narration about fungi media, evoking the dispersion of personal identities of the performers.

Digging into the layers of dirt in the Dungeons, I welcome the dark poetics of exhumation as a practice of understanding life via its obscure materialities – 'ungrounding of exhumation, breaking surfaces, distorting topologics of the whole, transforming the solidity of meaning into mushy mess, uncovering semi-life that is not determined by life forms that ferment' (Negarestani 2008, 59). Those messy investigations and explorations further deteriorate the social status quo of aesthetic and ethical values, symbolic systems of cultures and eventually also the continuity of linguistic expression. At the same time, the dynamics of hole complexities proposes some new forms of material arrangement, which Negarestani describes as follows: 'The abrupt escalation in pore triggers further and radical deformation of the solid matrix, dilatation and contraction of pores ..., progressive ungrounding of solidus, regional pore collapse and finally the composition of new worm-ridden spaces or zones of emergence' (59).

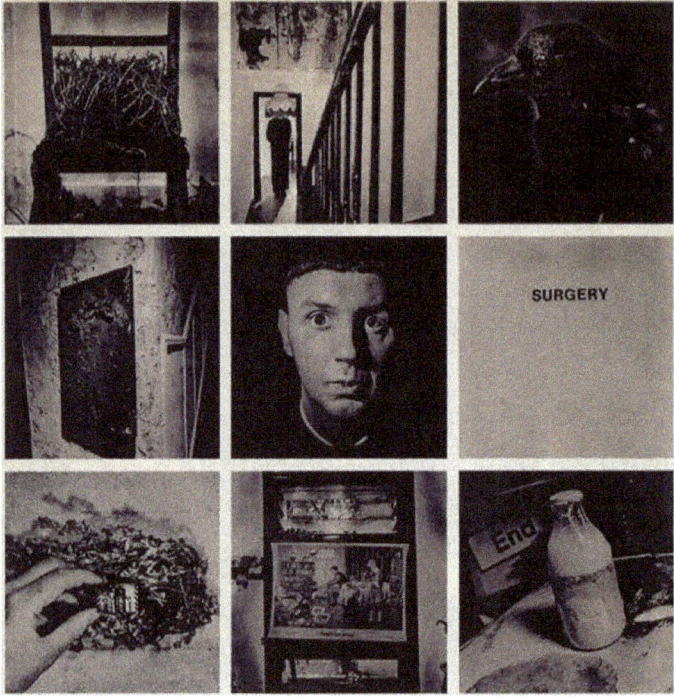

Fig. 11. The Institution of Rot (Richard Crow), 1994. Visual presentation of the space of the Institution of Rot in *TimeOut London* in 1994. Image courtesy of the artist.

The new zones and spaces in the Dungeons inevitably exhale from rot.

Strategically, the Institution of Rot art space (animated by Richard Crow) has assisted with the curation of the Chronic Illness of Mysterious Origin from the very beginning. This obscure Islington performance space originated from the occupation of a derelict tenancy in Holloway between 1992-2009, establishing itself in parallel to the Internet. Yet this dwelling of decay explored a very different idea of archives to that of computer databases. It was overgrown by plants, fungi and microbial colonies recording the performative actions through accompanying decomposition processes. 'In history as in nature, the rotten is the laboratory of life' (Institution of Rot 2023), says the motto of the Institution of Rot, a space which hosted live art explored as a practice of decomposition. Richard Crow, who runs the space, brought along his expertise of almost two decades of living amidst decaying architecture. His strategy was to re-enact the subversive potential of rotten spaces with persistent conceptual situations. He also became the prime infector of the Institution of Rot building. The rotten dust of the decayed dwelling became the key creative element for Crow. Within this domain of contagions and pollutants, the Chronic Illness of Mysterious Origin is a call out to the creative possibilities of dirt, dust and infectious sporulation, which Negarestani interrogates in their ability to mediate between drastically varied life formations. 'Dust particles originate from dark carriers never trodden before, different territories (fields of narration) and domains of invisible hazards' (Negarestani 2008, 88). They form complexities which are hard to analyse but which are also prone to rapid hybridisations and mutations.

The Institution of Rot brought an ethos of a rotten laboratory into the Dungeons, with its systematic investigation and dissection of decomposing anonymous materials, as well as its focus on anomalies of life, which often bear the stigma of illness. For Crow, 'the decaying entity becomes a laboratory slab upon which base-necrophilia (where death is infinitely deferred but progressively approached) is germinated' (Negarestani 2008, 185). Rot surprises us with new life given to materials that often hadn't even been recognised as living before. This life is as dangerous as it is unsettlingly vigorous, because 'it spawns more and more measures, micro scales, metronic cells, patches of solid, labyrinthine nexuses of dimensions, and wasteful dumps of scales' (Negarestani 2008, 186). Decay creates certain continuity in disintegration, as it collapses compositions, blurs the contrast between void and solid, breeds mushy disgusting softness and introduces anonymous ontology that eludes categorisation and sways towards the formlessness of nature, which precedes ontology. These and other forms of trans-organic disturbance are meant to dwell within the dusty Dungeons.

Dust offers a multiplicity and a conflicted diversity of life. It thus embodies a marvellous creativity, although it remains bonded to the emergence of plagues and diseased blasphemies. Dust feeds on the decomposition of human bodies (it often consists of dry skin), which many cultural systems repress by guarding and cursing the disposal grounds of their ancestor corpses. Nevertheless 'flesh is already a reeking catacomb of dust-compositions, drenched by deluges. It implies that dust carves niches into this catacomb into which to deposit all the bacterial data it has scavenged from wet milieus, xeno-chemical planes, interstellar dimensions and oceanic wastelands .... [F]lesh is a heap of data-pollution' (Negarestani 2008, 94). Negarestani invites us to see our bodies as composed of dust specks mediating untold material histories of life and the universe. What is offered here is an engagement in the playful experimentation with rot and an ambivalence of biological death, as 'Flesh is a dust necropolis, which is constantly refreshed by wetness, a necropolis full of cursed cemeteries, vaults of anonymous materials from the outside crypts and restless things' (94). The cryptic exhaust of crypts contains energetic intensities of dust, which carries myriads of bacterial and fungal entities. Those fungoids penetrate the bodies of mutant performers at the Dungeons, decomposing them into waves of Chronic Illness.

Negarestani notices that one ounce of dust contains more bacteria than there are people on the planet. Noticing this, he also points out that an invisible microbial universe infiltrates human bodies, unknowingly transforming them into transhumans, simply with 'a swarm particle creeping off the radar screen; a speck of dust you never know whether you have inhaled or not' (94). Moreover, the opening of the porous tissue of fungi, and the releasing of spores mediated by dust, are described by Negarestani as an exhumation of ancient microbe data. The dust-mediated sporulation can be recognised as a bacterial relic from the prehistory of life. Thus, our human bodies seem to be containers for the sedimentation of the biosphere's pastime. All of that accelerates the creative modes of life's perpetuation 'for decay cannot be captured as either formation or destruction' (182). Decay is not a definite death precisely because it perpetuates itself 'in order to indefinitely postpone death and absolute disappearance. In decay, the being survives by blurring into other beings, without losing all its ontological registers. In no way does decay wipe out or terminate; on the contrary it keeps alive' (182). This is also the ambivalence of the Chronic Illness' invasive cycles, which disturb the integrity of human bodies, but at the same time systematically open them up to the multiplicities of nonhuman life. Excessive proliferation of scales and forms that accompanies the processes of rotten decay and infectious illness meshes up the characteristics of the species, confuses taxonomies and transgresses the differences between individual organism, eventually levelling all life forms. '[C]orpses which had been of the same species when living might differ in species from one another when corrupted' (Negarestani 2008, 184). At the same time rot stimulates the sickly excessiveness of microbial mutation enacted by the Chronic Illness performers.

In the 'Directions for Decomposition' section of his *A Short History of Decay* E. M. Cioran proclaims that 'everything that breathes feeds on the unverifiable' (Cioran 1975, 10). The only certain thing is death. Life tries to win time by eluding certainty with the fruitful improbability of desire, or rot. In *Vibrant Matter* Jane Bennett begins from a similar conviction that the energy of life always escapes human ideas of certainty as expressed in knowledge-making that wants to control matter.

Nevertheless, she accentuates that humans share vitality with other forms of matter, to the extent that humans can be 'also nonhuman' (Bennett 2010, 4). The many intimate connections of humans with nonhuman creatures mingle all material forms within networks of shared vitality, 'vitality that persists even in trash' (6). There is no dead matter in Bennett's point of view, as she describes even the most degraded forms as inherently creative, possessing what she calls 'thing-power: the curious ability of inanimate things to animate, to act, to produce effects dramatic and subtle' (6). Rethinking the differences between materialities more horizontally by venturing into a gutter of civilisation can lead to encounters with forms of debris that are irreducible to culture. Such debris is nevertheless what the mutant performers enact during the Chronic Illness events by re-embodying bodily manipulations from online spaces. In this way, they enact a post-Internet corporeality in the physical space of the Dungeons.

In the context of self-organised squatting networks, I situate my Chronic Illness biomedia events as enacting an anti-ideological micropolitics of communal living with decomposing nonhuman life. Jean-François Lyotard's criticism of art, as outlined in his essay 'Notes on the Critical Function of the Work of Art', presents a decompositional approach to social organisation. Pointing to the fatal limitation of all political ideologies, Lyotard offers the ultimate form of open-ended politics. He proclaims, 'what is revolutionary is precisely to hope for nothing' (Lyotard 1984, 78). The sheer formal action of the dismantling of ideologies promises much more in its dynamic negativity than any positivism of new ideologies, as artistic deconstruction of human cultural constructs can be seen as a method of tapping into a broader context of life processes, he argues. Lyotard's strategy of artistic dismantling of ideologies is an example of an intuition in contemporary philosophy that explores the technological impact on human social organisations in terms of decomposition processes as well as in terms of the social co-existence of the species. Decomposition accelerates mutation through the diversity of chronic illnesses caused by various species living within and through each other. The curation of the Chronic Illness performance events brings the realisation about living through decay to the level of social organisation, where the most fertile form of communal living is offered by the anarchist undoing of politics and where humans have to find their nomadic homes in sewage.

3Decay

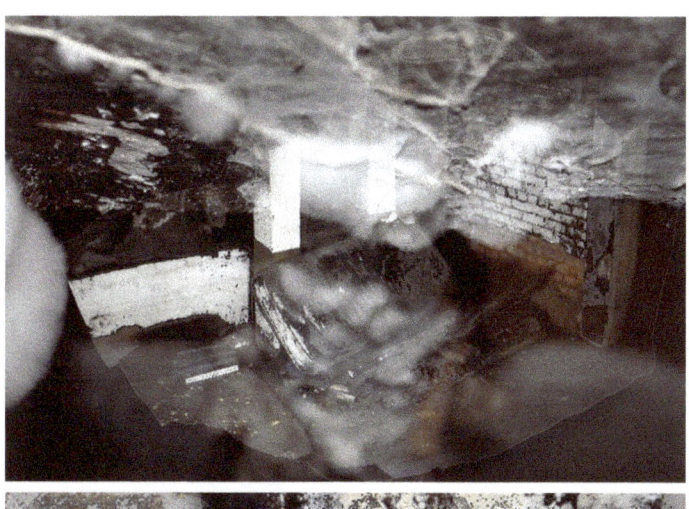

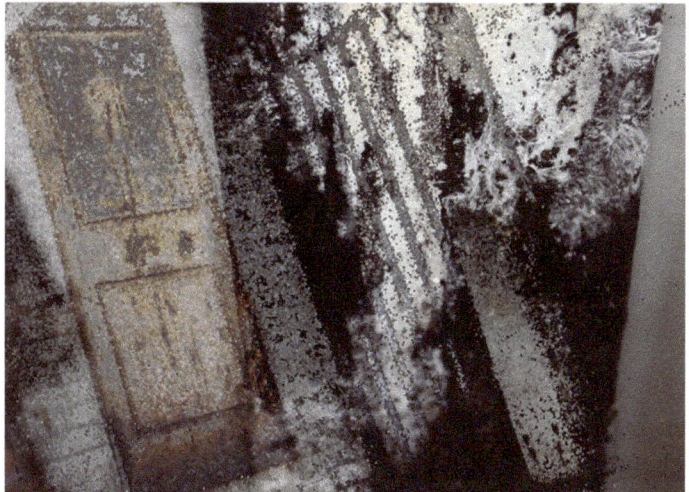

Figs 12-13. Piotr Bockowski, 2019. *3Decay* series, with technical assistance from NeonM3.

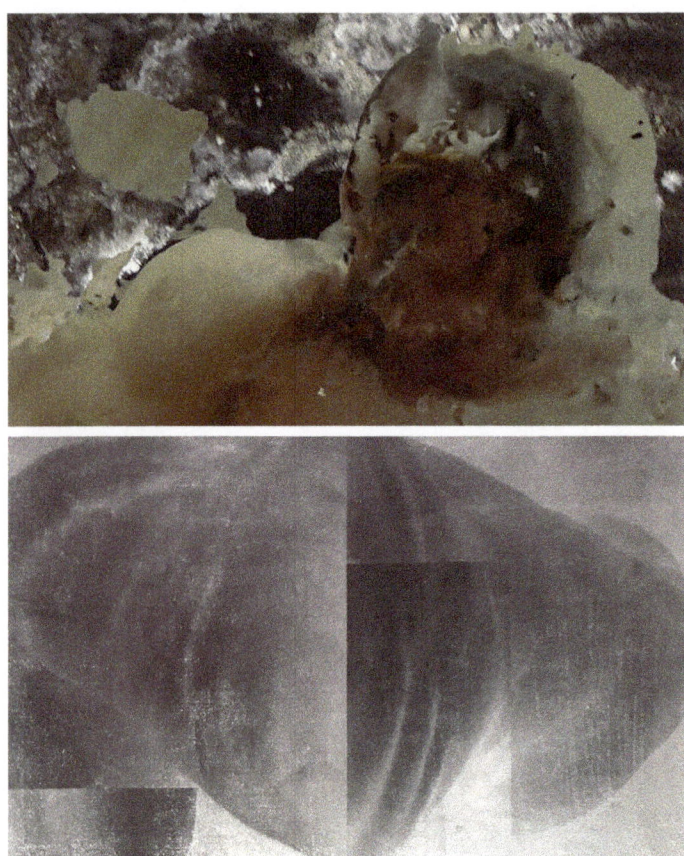

Figs 14-15. Piotr Bockowski, 2019. *3Decay* series, with technical assistance from NeonM3.

The Dungeons of Polymorphous Pan 183

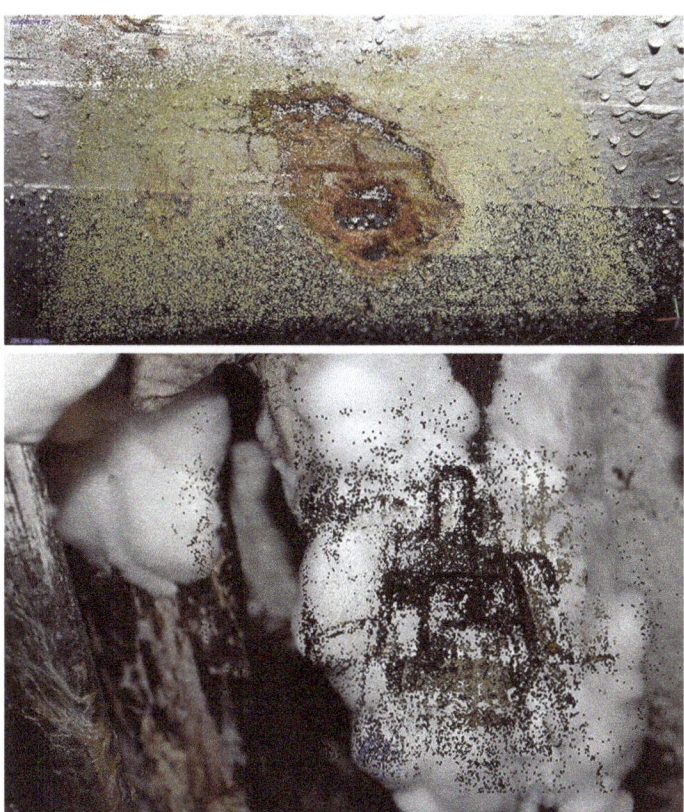

Figs 16-17. Piotr Bockowski, 2019. *3Decay* series, with technical assistance from NeonM3.

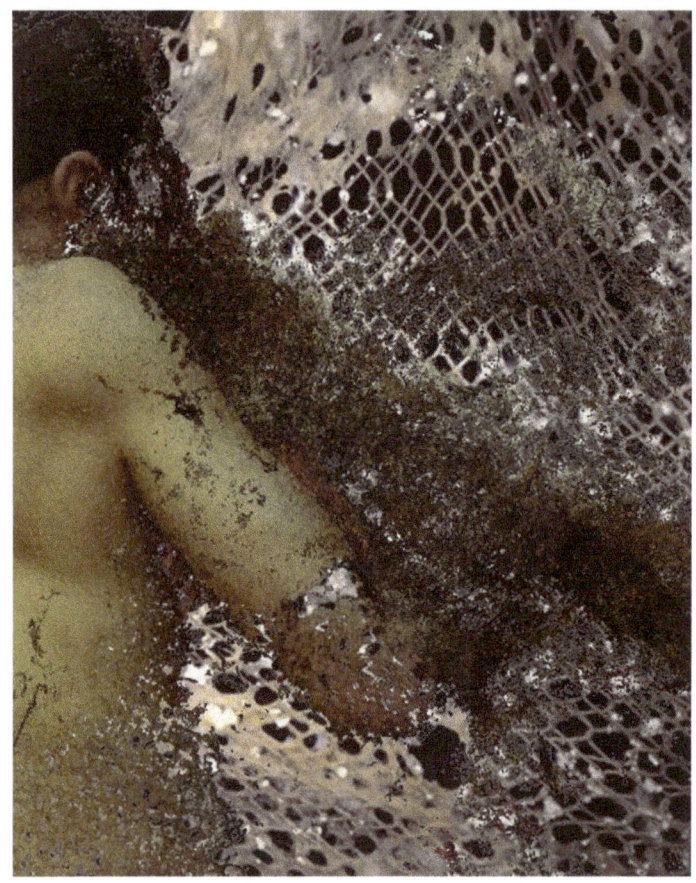

Fig. 18. Piotr Bockowski, 2019. *3Decay* series, with technical assistance from NeonM3.

The Dungeons of Polymorphous Pan

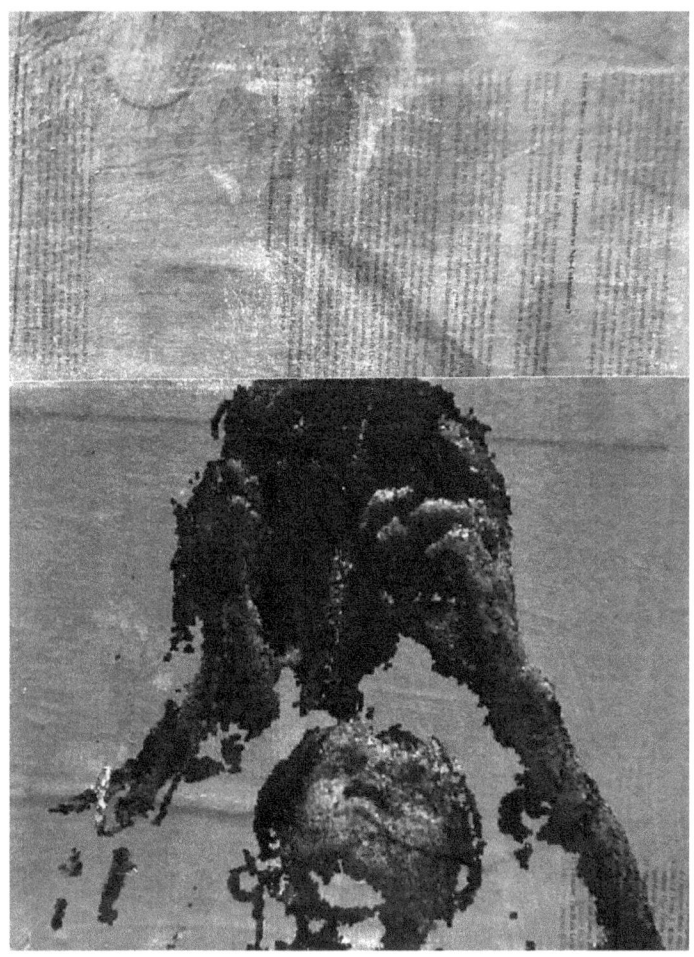

Fig. 19. Piotr Bockowski, 2019. *3Decay* series, with technical assistance from NeonM3.

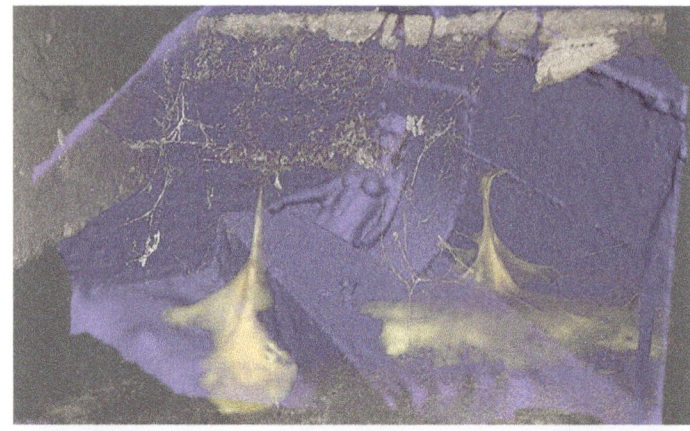

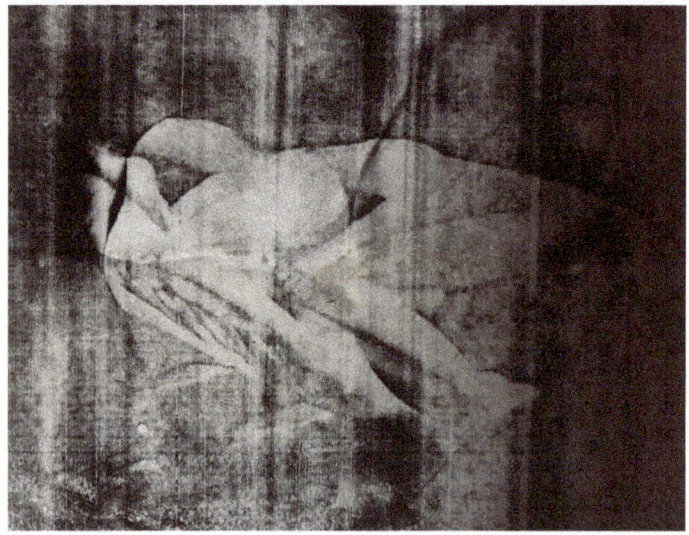

Figs 20-21. Piotr Bockowski, 2019. *3Decay* series, with technical assistance from NeonM3.

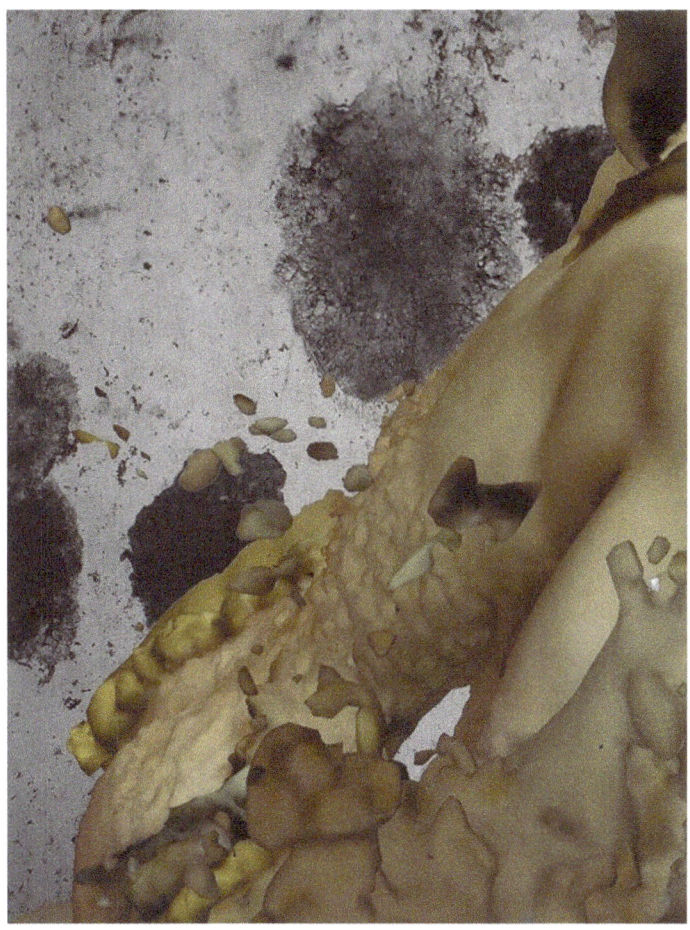

Fig. 22. Piotr Bockowski, 2019. *3Decay* series, with technical assistance from NeonM3.

Chapter 4

Fungosexual Replication Beyond the Internet

Biomedia

After my theoretical interrogation of the media concept of bodily decomposition (in Chapter 2) and the discussion around the embodiment of this concept in my own practice of the mutant performance as well as the curation of the Chronic Illness events (in chapter 3), I now want to consider various ideas regarding how humans reproduce their bodies via technological mediations, with bodily reproduction being arguably the superstructure of life. Primarily, we could say that the first chapter of this book conceptualised human media technologies as extensions of primitive life formations that still animate human bodies and environments. The concept of human bodily decomposition names different forms of mediation that open the idea and materiality of the human body to its transhumanist embeddedness in fungoid environments. Decomposition performed by fungal mediations disintegrates the humanist understanding of the performers' bodies and provides nourishing connections with nonhuman entities. My concept of 'fungi media' proposes a narrative of a creative devolution of the human species, where the creation aspect emphasises symbiotic relations of humans with other species. I suggest that, through the development of a high-tech civilisation, the human species encloses itself in a sphere of artificial conditioning that can be understood in its relation to fungoid life's organisation – rather than as something specifically human. In this sense humans undo themselves partially through their participation in electric media networks, as they experience and enact an increasingly more visible fragmentation, multiplication and hybridisation – of both their bodies and their subjectivities. Internet mediations of human bodies enmesh them with nonhuman entities and, as a consequence, open up ways of thinking about humans via nonhumans.

Exploring this idea through various forms of embodiment in post-Internet performance art Chapter 3 of this book has focused on my curation of performance events at the Dungeons of Polymorphous Pan, under the theme of the Chronic Illness [fig. 23]. Accounting for my own research practice, I have examined notions of trans-corporeal dynamics unfolding together with the space of live performance. Now, in the fourth chapter of this book I will offer a speculation, informed by strategies of bodily image manipulation unfolding online, on how media contribute to changes in human reproduction, involving a shift from sexual coupling to fungosexual replication. This shift will

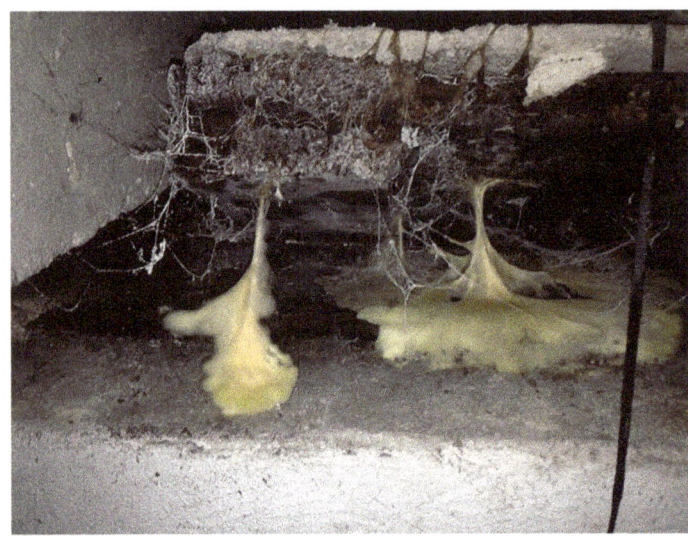

Fig. 23. Piotr Bockowski, 2019. Fungal media symerging life forms at the Dungeons of Polymorphous Pan.

allow me to further outline a framework of alternative queer, trans and nonhuman sexualities, which I am calling 'fungosexual'. Here, I am specifically interested in ways of extending online bodily manipulations into the corporeal processes of performance art, with a view to engaging nonhuman materialities of life. Pursuing this idea, it is vital to define media not only as material agencies that facilitate communication in an abstract sense (human and nonhuman) but also as living biological forms of corporeal transmutation that change our bodies into no-longer-human entities.

Media connect life forms, but at the same time they have always been more than passive technologies of communication or information storage. Looking at media in their peculiarly experimental form of bioart,

Robert Mitchell argues that media perform as material agencies, which make life forms grow and reproduce (Mitchell 2010, 96). Creating environments for the emergence of human and nonhuman hybrids beyond sexual reproduction, mediations come to life also as fungosexual mutations. I am particularly interested in interpreting human technologies of communication in terms of biomedia, which I consider as nonhuman forms engaged in reproducing no-longer-human bodies.

Bioart

As Mitchell points out, media are not only the material means of storing and transmitting information but also materials 'that are employed to keep living cells developing, dividing, and transforming' (Mitchell 2010, 11). Bioart is a 21st century hybrid art practice that explores the connection between those two understandings of media. Employing communication technologies and living organisms, together with various biotechnologies, it postulates a sense of life as 'a perpetual process of emergence' (Mitchell 2010, 11) beyond informational patterns. Based on his research into bioart, Mitchell formulates the concept of media vitalism that transgresses the understanding of media-as-communication and moves towards media-as-transformation, or transmutation, of matter, with a view to the possibility of merging both. Approaching media as conditions of bioemergence and generative vitalism, one has to see them not as artefacts or isolated processes but as living environments. Mitchell's vitalist media participate in life in a way that is irreducible to scientific laws or essentialist ideas. They 'explore what life can do' (Mitchell 2010, 32) instead of offering a fixed understanding of media – or of life. This experimental approach positions itself always one step ahead of the theoretical frameworks currently used by science. Approaching biotech outside corporate interests, media vitalism does not negate the validity of scientific research but rather performs life in the spheres and notions beyond scientific definitions. In this vitalist view of media that I also adopt and then perform myself, technology does not reduce life to the supposedly essential codes, algorithms or patterns. Instead, media are seen to replicate life in a new way. As an effect, the changing media may also be changing the environmental conditions, which in turn alter the living bodies inhabiting those environments or even create some new species (Mitchell 2010, 97). With this approach in mind, the Internet can be considered a transhuman form of life, with post-Internet performance art of body mutation being an embodiment of this aspect in parallel to bioart practice.

A paradigmatic example of bioart practice is the Tissue Culture & Art Project (TC&A) initiated by Oron Catts and Ionat Zurr in 1996 in Australia and 'set up to explore questions arising from the use of living tissues to create/grow semi-living objects/sculptures' (Catts and Zurr 2002, 365). TC&A use living biomaterials, sustained with engineered artificial support systems, in order to control the growth of the manipulated life forms and shape them into biotechnological 'semi-living sculptures'. Allegedly, the cells' compounds of TC&A's semi-life are molecularly (i.e., biochemically) altered but the results of their work are often presented in a form of 'digital montage'. In a way, a 3D computer-generated image becomes here not only a scaffolding for the growth of life but also its exoskeleton, shaping it inside out. The involvement of digital image tools in the performance of bodily mutation in media becomes for me a form of technological vitalism incorporated by Internet cultures. Exclusive high-tech academic experiments of bioart have offered aesthetic strategies related to the technological interrogation of bio-bodies that become the driving force behind mutant embodiments of humans, online and beyond.

Embracing, or rather allowing to be embraced by, the technological vitalism of bioart, the Officina Corpuscoli (Officina Corpuscoli 2023) studio in Amsterdam employs fungi for design projects that rethink human culture in the context of material processes of decomposition. Their Mycelium Shroud involves a human form, designed with an intention to understand life through cycles of physical decay and the resulting transformation of organic matter [fig. 24]. The shroud, having been inoculated with fungi mycelia, offers a mediation between a human body and a dispersed organic plateau connected to other forms of life. In doing so, Officina Corpuscoli is one of the many recent applications of fungi that focus on their body shapes, behavioural patterns or communicational possibilities in design. Other projects of Officina

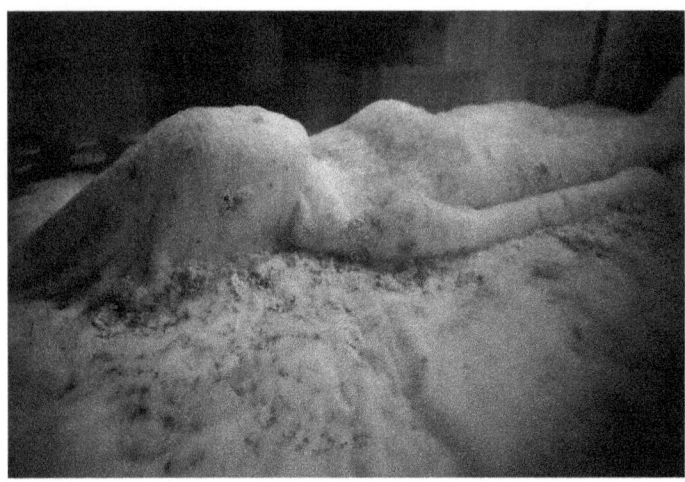

Fig. 24. Officina Corpuscoli, 2019. *Continuous Bodies – Bodies of Change – mycelium shroud with fungal growth.*
© Officina_Corpuscoli_Maurizio_Montalti.

Corpuscoli involve a spore-growing solution that could help humans develop a life-supporting infrastructure on Mars. This latter project accentuates the key role of fungi for biological environments and their kinship with humans in the high-technological age of cosmic expansion. Officina Corpuscoli defines a concept of 4D printing, which not only uses fungal bodies as a material for printing computer-based 3D designs but which, moreover, fuses algorithmic calculations with mycelial processes of growth. Their product design applications also include fungal-infected jewellery, as well as increasingly popular 'fungal leather' solutions for fashion and textiles, or self-devouring furniture animated by plastic-eating fungi, proposing an exciting solution to one of the main environmental pollutants created by human industry. Bringing back human civilisation to the material processes of nature is what the fungal approach to technology stands for. It significantly reverses the productivist approach to technology, which has been powering the industrial societies for the past couple of centuries, arresting the movement of life. In his commentary on Hannah Arendt, Bronislaw Szerszynski concludes that, via the fabrication of technology, humans remove material 'from the cycles of growth and decay' (Szerszynski 2003, 205). Bioactively redefining those most basic product ideas and the concepts behind technologies of production for the mass industry, Officina Corpuscoli represents the avant-garde of reversing the deadly impact of the consumerist civilisation on our planet. It does this by implementing the paradigm of fungi media premised on reconnecting to growth through decay.

Coming from a high-tech design research lab, the Mycelium Shroud elaborates on the becoming of the human form as a transient momentum of microbial processes. The ephemeral quality of fungal afterlife is presented by Eugene Thacker in his foreword to *Death, Mort, Tod* as a subtle touch point between the intimacy of information technologies and the primordial microbiology of 'elemental mud'. 'The result is a view of death as an impossible life that determines every life. Scaled up as clouds of numbers and patterns, sunken down in elemental mud. Weightless ash, sunken data' (Thacker 2018, 7), writes Thacker. His insight accentuates the decomposing performativity as the main characteristic of the body, rather than just a feature of a solid substance defined by vast technological artefacts. Interestingly, this performative affair of biodesign is reflected in the present-day tendency of performance art to be experienced intentionally via technologically elaborate 'reperformance' (Newman 2010, 231) simulations, video documentations, digitally manipulated imagery or even Virtual Reality systems. I would argue that those elaborations open up a new form of vitalism for human body acts. Advanced apparatuses, which have seemingly escaped from scientific laboratories themselves, become mutagenic life performances.

Media Mutations

The profound impact of the vitalism of new technological environments on humans increasingly involves human bodies in media-mutant performances. Arthur Kroker writes about a 'body drift' (Kroker 2012) that conceptualises 'the fact that we no longer inhabit a body in any meaningful sense of the term but rather occupy a multiplicity of bodies – imaginary, sexualised, disciplined, gendered, labouring, technologically augmented bodies' (Kroker 2012, 2). The mutant embodiment of media is characterised by the disintegration of human bodily identity.

Transhuman bodies online multiply unfinished processes, disperse intermediate stages of development, break apart organisms, perpetuate disconnected fragments and splice or decompose tissues in a non-regular manner. For Kroker this process is directly related to the 'effortless' circulation between the ever-growing forms of technological media. The bodies of techno-humanoids are characterised by a lack of coherence and by repeated becomings of performative transgressions. The price for the growing intensities of bodily performances is the unprecedented loss of the body's concrete materiality and material objectivity. 'Nothing is as imaginary as the material body. Circulating, fluid, borderless, with no certain boundaries or predetermined history' (Kroker 2012, 3). And yet that flux radiates a different material intensity. Together with technological mediations of the Internet, video, mobile phones or computer games, Kroker recognises this tendency also in the proliferation of countersexualities (4). In his view various androgynous sex codes, defined online as gender fluid, switch, transgender or nullo, for example, are a direct consequence of the changeability of techno-communication environments. Social media artist Salvia performs those different modes of post-sexuality in extreme mutant figurations that allow them to breed multiple oddkin bodies through acts of genitals erasure.

Salvia's digitally embodied performance art is arguably one of the more extremely unique and bizarre intensifications of 21st century media gravitation towards the presentation of androgynous bodies as the most intense expression of beauty, employed in mainstream culture by fashion editorials. In his presentation of this tendency, Patrick Mauries proclaims 'the dizzying resurgence of androgyny in the twenty-first century' (Mauries 2017, back cover) and adds:

'After all, the androgynes of the early decades of the twenty-first century are now flourishing in myriad incarnations, many of which did not even have a name only a few years ago' (Mauries 2017, 157). Salvia pushes this desire to erase sexual difference to its certain conclusion in visions of monstrous mutant breeding. This breeding process reaches beyond social media, towards experimental attempts at cross-species embodiments. In Salvia's early-pandemic fashion show, orchestrated together with the iconic curator and artist Parma Ham, the pair explored the body figure of 'nullo', defined as 'a form of body modification where the genitals and breasts are surgically removed' (Parma Ham 2019). For the show, they created fetishware and bodily augmentations consisting of multiple prosthetic tentacles, mammalia, twisted spines, exoskeleton tails and parasite ribcages. During the show the 'sissy slut s/s' models circulated around a gimp body disposed, and partially immobilised, like a lump of flesh, to be penetrated with a dildo made out of a taxidermised deer leg. This act of infertile self-proclaimed 'necro-bestiality', which incorporated hooves, horns, pig trotters and tentacles, was performed with an intention to 'reinvent' sexuality as posthuman 'practices to suit the needs of our imagined internet self which has begun to influence and inspire day-to-day experience' (Parma Ham 2019). Those excessive performances play with forms of dehumanised fetish organs that are attached to some actually desexualised bodies.

The characteristic of the phenomenon of mutant bodily performance, described by Kroker as body drift, is internally conflicted in its approach to the body. On the one hand, it diagnoses a certain 'dematerialisation' of human bodies through media, in the sense of dissolving bodies by making them more fluid or porous, but, on the other hand, the materiality of the mediated bodies is being intensified through their performativity, whereby various processes of technological transmutation create new mutant visceralities invading our culture. It takes 'a regime of computation' and 'the language of software as ideology' (Kroker 2012, 11), to borrow terms from N. Katherine Hayles, to create the accelerating multitude of media-simulated fetishes, which enforce the most peculiar sexual obsessions. Some counterculture critics of civilisation, such as John Zerzan, perceive the indulgence in the medial proliferation of body simulations as a pitfall of 'mediated high-tech dependency' (Zerzan 1994, 144) and of the enslavement of the raw pre-technological body. But perhaps there have never been humans, or any other living organisms, without a form of mediation of their bodies. The abstracted 'raw body' is therefore just an idea that has become detached from life processes.

Moreover, through the acts of Salvia and other mutant performers, such as Arca or Aun Helden, the elaborate media simulations become embodied anew in transhuman corporeal art inspired by online aesthetics. In his reading of Deleuze and Guattari's concept of the 'desiring machine' (Deleuze and Guattari 1983, 340),

Slavoj Žižek explains that the problem of the technological incarnations of human drives is not to reduce the mind to material processes (of the brain or computer system infrastructure for that matter) but 'to grasp how mind can emerge only by being embedded in the network of social relations and material supplements' (Žižek 2004, 16). This problem touches upon human identity, with its sexuality and subjectivity, and the way those characteristics rely on mechanical components and incorporate machines, or media technologies, which effectively positions the human sexual subjects as 'voided' by machines. 'It is meaningless to imagine a human being as a biological entity without the complex networks' (Žižek 2004, 19) of media, explains Žižek in his reconstruction of the concept of external intelligence, defining human momentum through its technological mediation. Humans are defined by their prostheses while, at the same time, the prostheses become part of the human's 'direct self-experience as a living organism – thus decentering us from within' (Žižek 2004, 18). It is a form of the fungoid external intelligence of heaps, networks and assemblages that becomes the living experience of humans online. Žižek calls this phenomenon the 'spectral materialism' (25) of human techno-body, explaining that it makes the 'material density in humid heaviness' disappear. The revolutionary paradigms of 20th century science are arguably leading to this 'spectralisation' of matter, which is what happens to the living bodily form of humans online. Informatics disperses objects into digital clouds, biogenetics abstracts organic tissue into DNA reproduction while quantum physics blurs matter into wave oscillations or reduces the reality perceived by human to 'quantum' – the neural processes of their neurobiology, points out Žižek. In his view the 'emphatic and ecstatic assertion of the body is thus over' (25), as the body loses density and becomes technologically manageable. The notion of 'spectral materiality' is strongly emphasised by mutant performers, such as Anthropomorph, as they proclaim their inhuman nature and intense affiliation with bestiality online – alongside their gender transitioning. They create elaborate silicon prosthetics to convey their transgression of human genders and other features of the human species, through the process of breeding hybrid bodies.

Arguably, communication seems to be a process that facilitates the making of all bodies. That may explain why technology in its many forms easily becomes a fitting container for the most primal human desires and drives – such as sex, violence and consumption. Humans also tend to fall for the erotic allure of media technologies, and from a certain perspective, 'bodily sex appears to be no more than an exchange of signal blips on the genetic corporeal network' (Heim 1993, 85), as suggested by Michael Heim in a chapter titled 'The Erotic Ontology of Cyberspace' in his book *The Metaphysics of Virtual Reality*. But then Heim concludes that VR, as a reductionist simulation of the body, unifies the possible bodily modalities of experience into mathematical patterns. By doing so, it does not satisfy the craving to penetrate (or be penetrated by) the physical reality, even though 'the fleshy world is worth knowing for its distances and its hidden horizons' (107), as Heim concludes. Technological simulations of transhuman bodies arrest sexuality in forms of detached ambiguity.

There is a flipside to the transgression of sexuality as a specific reproductive technique. Bio-reproductive sex facilitates cultural traditions via marriage and family institutions, but media technologies assist in dissolving them into a post-sexual excitement of mutating fetishisms. This technological undoing of human sexuality is particularly visible in queer subcultures, which, according to Myra J. Hird, behave like bacteria who 'recognise, and avidly embrace diversity, [as] they do not discriminate on the basis of sex or "gender" differences at all' (Hird 2004, 88)! The challenging of the sexual identity of humans in its core turns playful queer aesthetics into a radical political activity, as it abandons the self-similar replications of family lineages while embracing the symbiotic coexistence of different bodies.

Queer Politics via Biotech Aesthetics

Queer bodies are a form of mediation that is undoing the productivist ideology of political economy, according to Kroker (Kroker 2012, 27). Indeed, queer bodies are seen as weakening the social structuring orchestrated around sexual reproduction. Accordingly, Kroker not only associates queer bodies with non-normative sexual behaviours, but also finds them symptomatic or representative of other marginalised and excluded bodies.

Queer 'sex minorities' happen to be more than socially ostracised: they are sometimes lynched or even killed. In 2017 'at least 445 LGBT+ people in Brazil died in hate-related crimes' (Gasparini 2018, 55). This explains why Aun Helden, a mutant performer from the transgender community of Sao Paolo, wants to create a new form of existence for 'manas' (Brazilian slang for fem queers) by 'challenging the physiognomy of the human, by rejecting the aesthetic of "traditional beauty" and by breaking the rules of what is biologically possible' (Gasparini 2018, 55). Helden effectively transforms their multiplying body into reptilian creatures breeding eye-eggs through openings in latex membranes. In this way, they evoke a desired queer species apart from traditions of family culture.

Queer transgressions of human biological reproduction are guarded against by the rigid sexual dualism of many traditional cultures and punished according to repressive 'family values' that support the exclusivity of national or racial prejudices. Kroker links the ideological exclusion of sexual transgression with the techno-politics of 'body disappearance', which places refugees in trans-political camps, not marked on official maps (like Google maps) (Bauman 2004). A similar exclusion of socially obsolete bodies affects the one billion occupants, as estimated by Mike Davis, of the world's slums, bodies that make up the shameful underbelly of global economy (Kroker 2012, 52). As Kroker reminds us, the 'images of the very material body are everywhere – hostage bodies, bodies that are genocided, tagged, biochipped, surveilled and electronically scanned' (52). Against those forms of control enfolds the creativity of matter evident in vital approaches to media. Humans use media networks to form temporary dynamic alliances of wasted bodies that subvert their marginal social position by interpreting their stigma as a creative advantage. The initial meaning of 'queer' is 'rotten' and thus excluded, but at the same time infected by nonhuman fertility – which I will elaborate in a later section of this chapter titled 'The Humus of the Holobiont and Queer Rot'. Nowadays this 'queer rot' is widely applied by new media subcultures in association with culturally fertile activities, which are massively present in the mainstream culture of the Internet.

A spectacular performance of self-proclaimed 'mutants' of the Internet is offered by the queer mergence of the artistic entity of Arca and Jesse Kanda. These two artists met online in their early teens and developed a relationship in chatrooms commenting on 4chan (4chan 2023), a legendary otaku culture image-based bulletin board concerned mainly with Japanese media subcultures. It has a particular focus on fetishism, often involving extreme forms of sexual violence performed by animated monsters (one of the forerunners of 4chan was the Anime Death Tentacle Rape Whorehouse board – ADTRW). Coming from different continents – with Arca having grown up between Venezuela and the USA, and Kanda being of partial Japanese origin but living in multicultural Canada – they met in London after seven years of online co-development via the subtle touch of electronic media perversions. Arca and Kanda moved into a flat in Stoke Newington, an area in London renowned for its transgressive immigrant and dissident identity, historically being home to anarchists, abolitionists and other political non-conformists as well as religious outcasts, hosting the biggest Hasidic Ashkenazi community in Europe. In Victorian times those communities established themselves around the Abney Park cemetery, which is proud to be the first cemetery in the world for non-believers or otherwise religiously not affiliated. The website of Abney Park describes the origin of the place as 'the foremost burial ground for Dissenters – those practicing their religion outside the established church. It was founded on these principles, with a non-denominational chapel at its core, and was open to all, regardless of religious conviction' (Abney Park Cemetery 2023). Here Arca and Kanda tap into the socially subversive legacy, with the queer micropolitics fused with the mutant aesthetics of their media and performance art. They create a digital bodily entity consisting of 'fungus inspired' (Arca 2017) sound and visual deformations transforming each other's human features into monstrous overgrowth and spillage, as explained below.

In interviews around his album *Mutant*, Arca emphasises the experience of cruising in the Abney Park cemetery in front of their flat, where men have been meeting for dangerous sex since the Victorian times. In this cult graveyard of London queer subcultures, social outcasts had been buried for centuries and nowadays the exhibitionist desire of random sex encounters intertwines with the patterns of rot. In an interview about their work Arca is connecting queer eroticism with 'rot, which allows for different fungus and plants and insects to thrive there' and which creates 'textures of decomposition' (Arca in Petridis 2017) as another form of organic life. Arca's intention is to embody rot patterns with his sound distortions, as they explain their method of music making. Also, Kanda's computer image manipulations of Arca's body explore new prodigious forms of existence through media decomposition. Their fluid silhouettes severely challenge the integrity of organic structures but at the same time they allow animations of the infectious movements of plasmatic bodies to pulsate with life, spreading freely fine threads allegedly inspired by the growth in front of their flat by the entrance to the Abney Park cemetery.

Queer fertility is techno-mutagenic par excellence, as queers breed by shape-shifting their mediatised bodies. Abandoning sexual reproduction, they replicate via decompositions of their bodies within media environments. Bennet positions vital materialism as 'one great embryology' (Bennett 2010, 89) that seeks various new forms of replication in its 'pluripotentiality'. Accelerating in the 21st century, via the Internet and other platforms, mediated queer bodies offer new formats for group relations based on social media communications. They also create environs of techno-embryos for quirky breeds of fetishist performances: technologically generated processes of mediation of no-longer-human (mutant) bodies can be considered a form of breeding of queer progeny. This futuristic longing is expressed by Kroker in his prediction that 'the future belongs to those dwelling at the borderlines, to those who make of their bio-social-ecological abode the hybrid, the intermediation, the splice' (Kroker 2012, 27). Queer online culture can thus be said to produce simulations of posthuman technomutations.

Mutant Politics via 3D World-Making

Why do all these mutant bodies populate so many screens of computers connected to the Internet? Seemingly, there is a certain realisation behind the online art presented above that diagnoses digital media as increasingly mutagenic. The images discussed were mostly created in the year 2019, which witnessed a wave of censorship on major Internet platforms. Tumblr introduced their 'safe & trust' policies, involving the removal of pornographic and gore content, Vimeo started deleting many long-lived profiles after accusing them of 'activity primarily focused on sexual stimulation' and Facebook increased cases of blocking computer-selected profiles in the name of digital 'family values'. As part of that trend, many of my own blog posts related to the Dungeons of Polymorphous Pan were removed from public view. Three channels with almost one hundred videos of performance acts, produced throughout the past decade, were completely deleted, together with a couple of Chronic Illness social media accounts.

All those supposedly moral algorithmic systems behind the major social media websites nevertheless insistently convey an obsession with human sexuality. They aim at the suppression of a raw drive and desire that may appear aggressive. Trying to regulate the sexual expression of online communities, mainstream media policies effectively erase the imagery related to human bodily reproduction – the infamous nipples, shameful genitals or even more abstract body presentations that happen to involve moist or tense expressions, perhaps suggesting the possibility of secreting glands within hidden orifices. Those policies of familiar communities become uncanny as the mediated families insistently disconnect themselves from technicalities of sexual reproduction: they remove genitals, which are instrumental for creating an embryo; they also obscure female nipples, which are a characteristic of human motherhood (the word 'mom' [mother] originates from a Latin word for female breast – 'mamma'). Described above, the *Nullo* show of bestial castrations by Salvia and Parma Ham is a ceremonial presentation of aestheticised disability to perform human fertilisation. Another vivid example of a transgressive, corporeal rejection of bodily functions related to sexual reproduction was controversially enacted by eco and trans activist performer Bonnie Bakeneko [fig. 25], who removed their female breasts surgically and later ate their nipples during a live online transmission in 2019 (Bakaneko 2019). They did that partially as a gesture against the online prohibition against showing naked female

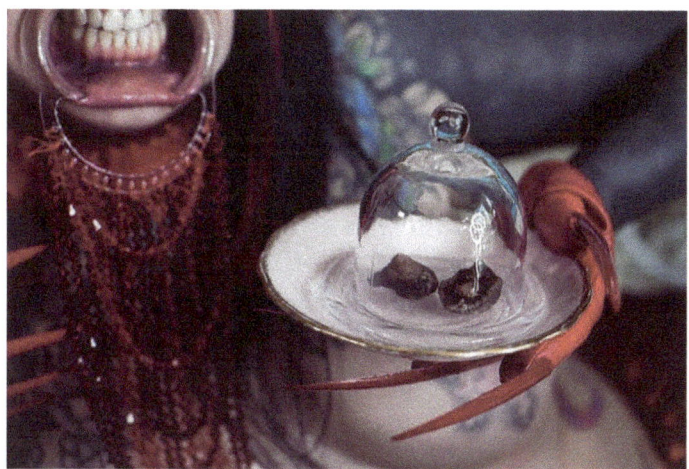

Fig. 25. Bonnie Bakeneko, 2019.
Online auto-cannibalism of female nipples.
Image courtesy of the artist.

breasts – with a particular fixation on female nipples. Enforcing the anti-genitals and anti-nipples censorship, the security systems of contemporary media populate the Internet with mutant replicants without nipples or genitals. Curiously, the Internet mainstream welcomes monstrous deformities as long as they escape the biological features of human sex. These problematic body-image policies assist in the coming of age of 21st century post-Internet mutant performers.

This fetishist spillage of repressed desire online taps into the Japanese *hentai* strategies of eluding censorship. Almost half a century old, they can be considered symptomatic of Internet aesthetics now. Since the 1970s Ero Guro movement in Tokyo, *hentai* has answered to the state prohibitions on portraying human genital intercourse by creating a fertile subspecies of tentacled monsters that twist around the no-longer human bodies and penetrate their dislocated orifices gaping in-between feverishly multiplying mammillae. In the same vein, mutant body performers on viral social media such as Aun Helden use their image manipulation art to castrate sex or 'anything that presents (them) as men' (Gasparini 2018, 55), at the same time multiplying what are considered to be anatomical anomalies. 'The eggs, the prosthetic make-up, it's a contrasexual decontextualization, it's a prosthetic incorporation. It's me playing with my body, displacing its origins and maybe replacing them' (Aun in Crooked 2019), teases Aun. Instead of harmonizing with human forms, their corporeal members bulge with black eggs that initiate a no-longer-human replication. The shiny surface of the eggs reflects the mutagenic void of computer screens that opens up to protosexual transmissions beyond cultural traditions.

Transcultural Sexuality

The aesthetic sexuality of fetishism is abstracted from bioreproductive functions and introduces cultural practices of sadomasochism and fetishism, which historically produce new forms of desire, according to the cultural analysis of Roman Byrne (Byrne 2013, 5). This process branches from the cultural phenomenon of pornography, which, according to Camille Paglia, can be recognised as one of the oldest forms of ritual and art (Paglia 1991, 34), thus establishing the primary reference point for body art. At the same time, Susanna Paasonen's (Paasonen 2011) research into online porn emphasises a strong relation of the phenomenon of pornography to the Internet, particularly in its fetishist and bizarre forms. Proclaimed as the very reason for the Internet's existence, porn is for her one of the integral parts of online economy or even 'an engine driving development in media technologies' (33). It not only makes many Internet users 'spend considerable amount of time masturbating by their screens' (32) but also, as an economic factor, 'the porn industry [has] played a crucial role in its [Web's] development as a commercial and largely audiovisual medium' (33).

Paasonen asks how the online economy orchestrated around the images of human bodies influences those bodies. She defines this influence around the modalities of viscerality and excess. Those modalities do not refer to the fixed structures of meaning but rather to the 'visceral resonance' (15) that bypasses analysis. As porn consumers are 'moved bodily before consciously processing what such experiences ... may mean' (15), a 'gut reaction' becomes a mode of engagement with the Internet, which has sensory and affective resonance, such as fascination or revolt. This state of events, in my view, constitutes an argument for the biological (i.e., physiological) character of the Internet, as opposed to it being seen primarily through the logic of the binary code behind computer programs.

Paasonen's concept 'points to the material factors of porn – the fleshy substance of the human body'

(20) as well as to the materialities of technology, such as hardware, cables and modems. Those bodily factors are mobilised by online porn through forms of shock, disturbance and non-symmetry. 'Online porn is indeed often irregular and strange, and it aims to stand out through the novelty of the desires, kinks, and displays of bodily pliability that it showcases' (Paasonen 2011, 20). Paasonen argues that the qualities of filth, disgust and nastiness or sickness resist domestication and support the intense attractiveness of porn for many Internet users. According to Paasonen's research the proliferation of niche online porn categories gravitates towards disgust and undoing of culturally-erected categories. One of the examples analysed by Paasonen is the viral popularity of coprophagia, which mixes the biological functions of different human orifices. Paasonen describes the video *2girls1cup* that presents an act of eating the faeces of one girl by another, who then vomits it into the other's mouth. Disgust related to that video is apparently 'primarily oriented towards embodiment and especially the excessively carnal – whether rotting flesh, sexual abundance' (211). The aforementioned excess of life, mutant procreation and the microbial decay of excrements are placed by Paasonen 'at the heart of the disgusting as bodies are entered, exited, and consumed' (211). Arguably, such acts evoke the pre-human evolutionary forms of life via the performative mergence of defecation, eating and reproductive (sexual) functions within one and the same orifice. This illustration of online porn's tendency shows that imagery

associated with human reproduction in network media context is meshed with images portraying processes of digestion. The close proximity of reproduction and digestion possibly suggests their common origin in the endosymbiotic relations between microbes.

Moreover, Paasonen notices that the porn videos that circulate between Internet users the most are 'extreme and bizarre, and sexual arousal generally plays a minor role in the titillation they evoke' (210). Interestingly, the peak performance of online porn is devoid of sexual arousal, according to her. This is yet another iteration of the decoupling of sexual behaviours from sexual functions, which arguably points to the beyond-sexual replication offered by new media via oversaturated simulations of sexy performance. Abject bodily forms proliferate on the Internet, while 'pornographic styles and gestures are circulated in so-called mainstream media (for example in advertising and music videos), and hardcore pornography is an increasingly accessible and mundane part of the media landscape' (Paasonen 2011, 248). The shock modality of porn becomes a feature of its liveliness in the technological environments of new media, especially in acts that play with excrements, which are decaying parts of human bodies and live microbial entities. Online performances of sexuality are decoupled from reproduction and tend to be disassociated from genital display and action. The omission of the very human techniques of sexual reproduction invites excitement of the fetishist reproduction of body images.

Online porn pursues bizarre bodily forms. New media imagery often tends to blend male and female beauty figurations into postsexual abstract hybrids, while approaching impossibly exciting monstrosities beyond sexuality. The abandoning of 'beauty standards' in queer subversions unexpectedly invites the horror of bodily mutations to creep in beyond the theatre of sex.

The Primordial Origin of Transsexuality

Psychoanalysis offers a monstrous hypothesis which locates the origins of humankind in cannibalism (Royle 2003, 208). In Freud's speculation, the totemic prohibition on eating each other precedes the incest taboo and, through placing a restriction on the pleasure of consumption, it constitutes the primal sexual relation of social hierarchy. In this quasi-mythological narrative (Freud 1919), cannibal savages killed and devoured their father, and thus established their community guidelines for sexual consent on the basis of that act. Disturbingly, this terrible fairytale bears an uncanny resemblance to the endosymbiotic theory of evolution developed by Lynn Margulis. In her widely acclaimed research (Margulis and Sagan 2000), Margulis proposes that sexuality as a biological technique of reproduction, characterised by the partial mixing of the genetic material of two parents that blend together half-way through a generational cycle, originates from the crisis of the primordial cannibalism of ancient bacteria. Those confused microbes that tried to devour each other, after reaching a state of overpopulation in relation to the natural resources that were available at the time, probably failed to digest one another completely and were forced to merge into new chimerical entities. Endosymbiosis proposes a theory of evolution which is driven by partial incorporation of many bodies converging into more complex clusters. Similarly, Frank Ryan's theory of virolution (Ryan 2009) posits that viral microbial agents are at work during human conception and perhaps animate the first splitting of fertile cells in women's wombs. Ryan rephrases the suggestion that the sexual nature of humans, in the context of the diversity of life on the planet, is neither male nor female but rather trans. This is the very broad, pre-sexual understanding of transsexuality that I adopt in my own work. I want to acknowledge that the term 'transsexuality' is nowadays considered by many in the trans community to be outdated or even offensive due to its medical and stigmatising associations, as it is seen to be pointing to the seeming disparity between one's biological sex and one's gender. Preference is thus frequently given to more inclusive terms, such as 'transgender' or simply 'trans'. Nevertheless, in my writings and practice I want to make a nod to the historical aspect of the trans debate, and to its associations with not just sex but also sexuality as always already being a process of transition. Yet I rename it 'fungosexuality' to emphasise its primordial character related to the various forms of the replication of fungoids, which, from the perspective of human reproductive sexuality and its binary structuring, should be considered androgynous, trans or otherwise bizarre. All of those categories are repeatedly referenced by post-Internet mutants in their performances of hybrid, alien bodies.

Alien transsexual entities of microbes, which are now incorporated within human bodies, seemingly create those bodies, then also reproduce and support the temporal integrity of their identities, such as familiar sexualities shaped by cultural traditions. Nevertheless, the contemporary impact of technological communications on cultures speeds up the erosion of the traditional values and makes it ever more apparent that the identities mentioned have 'to be performed over and over again' (Vecchi 2004, 16), which is something that is related to the lack of consistency and continuity of human identities over time. Since 'the frailty and forever provisional status of identity can no longer be concealed' (Vecchi 2004, 16) due to the withdrawal of social structures that used to produce the illusion of stability of traditional identities – now challenged by technology – humans are subjected to processes of 'corrosion of character' and experience 'profound anxiety'. Taking this lack of stability into account, Nicole Seymour proposes that the very loosening of identities can be translated into advantageous queer strategies of trans-identity which involve gaiety, irony and frivolity. Those strategies may prove themselves crucial in seeking solutions to the contemporary issues related to the environmental crisis. Less-than-humans of decomposed identities open up, according to her, to 'improper affiliation' (Seymour 2019, 115) of playful performance with other forms of life, instead of defining the deadly serious truths about them. Queer performance accentuates the performativity of the natural environment itself. Attentiveness to the capacity of some alien bodies affecting other transforming bodies brings closer 'the idea that nature or the environment could perform, be performed, or be otherwise constructed – rather than being immanent, palpable, or manifest' (Seymour 2019, 118). Those constructs can be considered as a form of the technological mutation of humans via their new media, performed instead of sexual reproduction.

Describing her male-to-female transitioning, lasting over two decades and involving surgical sex reassignment, Claudine Griggs accentuates the crucial role of education in modes of expression and the repeated performative acts that define her new gender. She also admits that that prolonged time of female gender performance still could not undo the imprint of having been reared into male gender identity. Effectively, Griggs' testimony of trans performance becomes a story of life through sexual and gender ambiguity. 'A person who is sexually unclassifiable gains the strangest rebuke' (Griggs 1998, 14), she concludes and explains that feminine men and masculine females get reprimanded by society and urged to choose their one 'consistent' sex, to end the ambiguity of 'transitioning'. Interestingly, the culturally transgressive aspect of media networks comes into play as it accelerates sexually ambiguous imagery. Griggs compares mid-'70s (the time of the beginning of her transitioning) with the late

'90s (the time of the writing of her book) as far as perception of gender in the USA is concerned. In the earlier days, the superficial element of 'female' looks was enough to define somebody as (or provoke an assumption about somebody being) a woman. After the arrival of the Internet, sexually ambiguous 'androgynous looks are common and don't define gender anymore' (Griggs 1998, 19). This transition opens up new cultural forms in the 21st century, when media embrace ambiguity and celebrate androgynous bodies that defy sexual stereotypes. Gordene Olga MacKenzie makes a valid point by stating that media culture not only creates the desire to consume androgynous images, but also that transgender may actually even be referred to as a 'condition tailor-made for our surgical-technological age' (MacKenzie 1994). Media mutations and biotechnology both embrace sexuality *and* gender in transition. Their crossover is particularly fertile for my work. In my performance practice outlined in Chapter 3 I deliberately engage with mutant aesthetics, which is moulded by the shapeshifting potentialities of the body. The *Synthetic Organs* act develops with the self-discovery of the body to be infected by alien entities, whereas in *Holobiont, a* biomedia installation performs fungoid decomposition as a strategy for the nonsexual replication of the human bodily image. Those acts establish my understanding of sexuality in terms of a fungosexual relation to nonhuman life.

Transsexual decomposition and an intimate self-remodelling of bodily features were exercised throughout the 'Pandrogeny' project of Genesis P-Orridge and Lady Jaye. They became mutilated during a fire at a music studio in LA in the mid-'90s and the medical insurance money they got was put to financing a series of plastic surgeries. The repeated surgeries were performed with an intension to make them look alike and through this process achieve a hybrid form of body mediation between genders. 'There is no gender anymore – only androgyny' (P-Orridge 2006a and b), said P-Orridge, and 'sexuality is the force of nature and cannot be contained' (P-Orridge 2006a and b), they added.

The *Pandrogeny Manifesto* video (later uploaded to YouTube) starts with a realisation that the human body is a host for DNA that is nonhuman, functioning as 'merely an environment in a symbiotic relationship with it' (P-Orridge 2006a and b). Genesis P-Orridge used the medical techniques of cosmetic surgery as well as online video manipulation to achieve both a prehuman and posthuman recombination of sexual characteristics. The blending of bodies was, according to them, evolutionarily advantageous. 'Destroy gender. Destroy the control of DNA and the expected. Every man and woman is a man and woman' (P-Orridge 2006a and b), proclaimed Lady Jaye just before showing the footage of Jaye and P-Orridge's face and breasts surgery in the second part of their video manifesto. They perceived the annihilation of the sexual dichotomy as expanding the view of evolution. In their book *Nonbinary*, Genesis P-Orridge elaborates on their idea of Pandrogeny they had been developing since the beginning of the 1980s. They write: 'the universe is made up of one kind of matter – everything. There is no binary universe. So there is no binary body' (P-Orridge 2021, 313). They proclaim mutation as the 'law of evolution' and associate it with art, creation, new ideas [and] experiments' (275) that are suppressed by control in human societies. The intention of the performer is to transgress the binary sexuality in order to achieve an unrestrained mutant reproduction of hermaphroditic bodies. During the process of 'ending gender' and 'breaking sex' (P-Orridge 2021, 318) their aesthetic intention was also to communicate with the nonhuman entities within their body in an attempt to detach from the human characteristics of this body.

No-Longer-Human Reproduction via Technological Decomposition

The fungoid 3D project, which I have presented right before this chapter, interrogates the vitalist understanding of communication technologies via my concept of fungosexuality, particularly through its relation to biological reproduction. The utilitarian applications of human technology do not exhaust its meaning, which is evident in the dual understanding of the term 'media' – as infrastructure to communicate information as well as materialities actively involved in the growth and reproduction of life.

The processes of the media decomposition of human bodies, which I discussed in Chapter 1, analyse the technological mediation of the bodies on the Internet in terms of bodily implosion. They are visions of disintegration leading towards corporeal mutations. The supposed technological extensions are invading human bodies and renegotiating their inner constitutions, 'as we realise how close technology is to the body or how deep it already is inside the body' (Kac 2005, 227), according to artist Eduardo Kac. As technology intertwines with life processes inside human bodies, it opens up the possibility of technological replication that performs beyond sexual reproduction by means of the invasion of technology into the bodies, and by reassembling those bodies from within.

In my practice I use 3D scanning with an intention to expose the intimate and necessary biotechnological manipulations of digitally embedded fungoids, which enter the body of the performer. Drawing on Eugene Thacker's *Biomedia*, I recognise technological mediations not only as material agencies that change human bodies but also as alternatives to sexuality. Biotechnology and advanced media technologies define the limitations of sexuality as reproductive technique and suggest other methods of bodily reproduction. The multiple phenomena of rotten queer media, together with the concepts of fungosexuality they convey, come along in human cultures as vectors of transgression of sexual reproduction. It could be argued that media invite forms of reproduction for the human species that go beyond sexuality. The theory of biomedia thus presents a challenge to the cultural formations based on fixed sexual identities.

In her comprehensive (yet not uncontroversial) cultural critique, Paglia investigates a great array of transsexual expressions from the mythology, through religion, theatre and art, all the way to literature of what she describes as 'western culture'. Her concept of sexual personae (Paglia 1991) offers a reading of human nature and civilisation as contextualised by the perpetual transformation of sexuality between male and female – and beyond them. She proposes 'transsexualism' as a wider context to understand the concept of sexuality in human cultures, particularly the 'western' cultures sprouting from the root of ancient civilisations. Commenting on the ancient Greek civilisation, she gives plenty of evidence for the transsexual character of the major mythological gods, linking it with the origin of the term 'technology' in the androgynous cult of Athena, who embodies 'the mind as techne, pragmatic design, [that] was hermaphroditic for the ancients' (Paglia 1991, 85).

Technology is introduced here as a survival modality for human bodies that exchange and shift the shapes of their sexual characteristics. Tied to the development of technology, the pursuit of science bears for Paglia the alchemical concern with the search for the perfect mutable substance. In alchemy, the primal form of matter and the matrix of life 'was depicted as an androgyne, aregis ("double thing") or as "chemical marriage" of brother and sister in incestuous intercourse' (198). This vision of primordial nondifferentiation gives Paglia an insight into the ever-transforming human nature, entangled with the techniques of transsexual morphs which precede sexualities of choice and eventually undo them. Thacker's biomedia also rediscover technology in the similar notions of the return to life's breeding 'swamp' beyond sex, 'teeming with monstrous prehuman mud creatures' (Paglia 1991, 324), as media technology enters the body of humans and is gradually understood as an integral part of their biology.

The theory of biomedia invites the conceptualisation of bodily entities that are shaped through the computer-networked performances of the technologically dehumanised body and that are capable of transindividual replications. In biomedia, not only is 'the traditional "wet lab" of molecular biology ... being extended, augmented, and even replaced by the "dry lab" of bioinformatics and computational biology' (Thacker 2004, 2), but also, conversely, the computational processes appear as 'wet' media again. According to Thacker, 'biomedia are particular mediations of the body, optimisations of the biological in which "technology" appears to disappear altogether' (6). What he describes here is actually the reversal of the 20th century obsession with the disappearance of the body into technology into the 21st century revelation of the disappearance of technology into the body. Inspired by the 1980s Californian proto-Internet subculture of 'cyberpunk' computer geeks and hackers, the term 'cyberspace' (Gibson 1984) describes a utopian realm of technological disembodiment, which is characteristic of the imagination of cybernetics. Cyberspace, associated in the 1990s with the Internet, established across the global mass media culture a popular assumption about the immateriality of computer-based communication and the new form of intelligence that it conveys, rooted in the famous 'Turing Test' (Lee 2006, 31). The test challenges human intelligence, suggesting that a computational machine will reproduce it once the machine is able to have a computer interface-mediated conversation with a human and will not be recognised as nonhuman by the human. Kihan Lee points out that the Turing Test assumes that intelligence is a disembodied phenomenon as it reduces human identity to language. This assumption is also deeply rooted in cyberpunk imagination, represented by Case, the protagonist of William Gibson's novel *Neuromancer*. Case forgets to eat, uses a chemical toilet in front of his computer and, in the critical moments in which he 'is engrossed in his work within cyberspace, his EEG is flatlined, in what amounts to 'out-of-body' experience. In a word, it is during moments of physical death that Case seems to be most alive in cyberspace' (Lee 2006, 31).

Cyberpunk's disregard for the 'meat' of human corporeality inspired fantasies of abandoning 'the prison of the flesh' in the proto-Internet subcultures of the 20th century. Now, the 21st century 'post-Internet' culture concerns itself increasingly with the impact of computer-based communication on human bodies and their environments, like the impact of one's lifestyle on health, the involvement of embodied situations in computational processes or the key role of the technology industry and energy consumption in the climate crisis, species extinction and the exhaustion of natural resources, as well as the role of the media in establishing the current global political regimes (USA, China or Russia) and the systematic exploitation of the global poor. There is no body-anxiety of transcending 'the meat' into virtual spaces anymore, as people have to deal with the growing avalanche of problems related to the embodiment of 'cyberspace'. Digitisation is considered inasmuch as the digital context changes the understanding of the biological, argues Thacker. Digital media have to be situated in the still wider corporeal context. This consideration finds its quintessential expression in the post-Internet art of mutant performers, who 'incorporate cyberspace' by mediating it through their bodily processes.

Thacker comments on the post-Internet civilisation of biomedia by presenting all of the human historical activity, on different levels of abstractions, as biotechnology. He suggests that 'In earlier techniques such as animal breeding or fermentation, the literal meaning of the term biotechnology is indeed this technical utilization of biological processes toward a range of novel ends' (Thacker 2004, 21). Thacker perceives all human historical (civilisational) activities in terms of the technological recontextualisation of biological components and processes. This important realisation, which I would like to mobilise for my own purposes here, is that even the most abstract dimensions of technology offer material contexts for human bodily performances.

Thacker promotes an understanding of biomedia that goes beyond the concept of the 'simulation' of the biological body with bioinformatics tools. Instead, he encourages us to see biomedia as different kinds of materialities that act together with other biobodies. Post-Internet mutant performance art embodies this important shift in the cultural understanding of technological civilisation.

Mutant Performance as Biohacking

Technology does not replace the biological body with simulations, explains Thacker. Digitalisation is not something separate from bodily performance. Bioinformatics, that is biological processes fused with computational technologies, formulates the context for the body enveloped, as essential data, by different technological patterns of relationships. Bioinformatics is widely applied in medicine to quantify the processes of the human body and measure their regularities. Bioinformatics manipulates complex biological data such as genetic codes. One of the most famous biotech research initiatives of the past century was the Human Genome Project (1990-2003). It attempted to pinpoint the relations between the configurations of biochemicals in cells and the self-making of human bodies – but it did not yield any definitive results. An even more intriguing follow-up is the ongoing Human Microbiome Project (2008-now), which examines the genetics of the vital multitude of 'microorganisms living in association with the human body' with a lookout on human health and disease, at the same time establishing the genetic understanding of humans as no-longer-human, since humans are essentially seen as being dependent on the massive support of nonhuman life forms. The computer manipulation of biodata in both projects nevertheless has to be positioned within the context of biology. Therefore, even the most abstract techniques of decoding the body do not abandon it. The techno-body 'is also a rematerialized, rebodied body' (Thacker 2004, 22).

In order to describe further the 'rebodied body' of biomedia, Thacker proposes the categories of 'the postvital' and 'the postnatural'. He considers human-designed receptor proteins that let pass only certain types of biomolecules, those whose shape fits the 'microbe orifice', as biomedia. Eventually, he uses the example of respirocites, i.e., specially designed techno-blood cells that deliver more oxygen to the human body. The other example are DNA motors – nanomachines that use DNA biochemicals in their structure as well as energy source. Those two examples represent the categories of the postvital and the postnatural. Postvitalism embraces the technovitality of programmable matter. It offers a vitalist stance for biotechnology against the reduction of life to coding. Postnaturalism, on the other hand, emphasises the embodiment of information in molecules. This corporeal practice of information makes a point that even the most abstract computational technologies have diverse bodily gravity on invisible scales.

Complexities of the technological body emerge from the microbiological plateaus, although not as 'generated' by the DNA code but rather as performed on the cellular level of living organisms. Thacker describes the organismic body as compared to the bioinformatic body. The description answers to 'three issues: the generation or origination of the living system, the adaptive modes of self-regulation of a living system, and the dynamic exchange of matter and energy of living systems as open systems' (Thacker 2004, 150). Those issues are defined in microbiological terms by sickness as a qualitative distinction of a biological open system. It seems that the very possibility of sickness defines the individual separation of biological complexity (such as the human) from the horizon of the open perspective of interconnected microbial networks. This very horizon of microbe events defines nonhuman bodies as indeterminately changeable. 'It forms a radically "other" model of the body, emerging from the predominantly technical orientations of systems biology, a model we have been calling the biomolecular body' (Thacker 2004, 163). Here, the abstraction of communication technologies does not get rid of the corporeality of media but once again refines it into the superdiversity of the miniscule scale. Just looking at random bacteria, we can find more than a thousand genes in each organism, which under proper conditions can change to a completely different species in a few seconds (Sharp 2015). The excessive diversity of life unfolds against the corpo-scientific techno-ideologies that want to control life through abstract unification theories. Basic embodied participation in the world serves as a critique of theoretical reductionism, something that was cogently articulated by Franz Kafka in the following terms: 'Now the world is known, however, to be uncommonly various, which can be verified at any time by taking handful of world and looking at it closely. Thus this complaint at the uniformity of the world is really a complaint at not having been mixed profoundly enough with the diversity of the world' (Kafka 1961, 41).

With this, Kafka proposes a strategy against the homogenisation of the perception of the world. He encourages us to enter and taste the world, in order to mix with its radical diversity. This approach seems to be performed by the 21st century subculture of young outcast biotechnologists from the MIT, with offshoots in San Francisco and NYC. Called 'biopunks' by Marcus Wohlsen in his book of the same title (Wohlsen 2011), they intend to 'hack the stuff of life' by setting up DIY wet labs in their homes, using cheap technologies constructed from basic devices, which they order from the Internet and repurpose to serve functions analogous to the extremely expensive high technology of enormous corporations. Their attitude is that, most of the time, biotechnology is fundamentally no different to cooking. Through this they effortlessly engage with the hidden but most powerful forces of life.

The attitude of biopunks is playfully adopted by Jake and Dinos Chapman's iconic sculpture *Zygotic Acceleration. Biogenetic De-Sublimated Libidinal Model*

(Enlarged x 1000). The sculpture moulds incomplete but amassed bodies of children into posthuman clusters of abjection, encapsulating 'a host of contemporary societal fears (such as) paedophilia, the sexualisation and exploitation of young children, biotechnology, cloning and medical research without boundaries' (Fortenberry, Morrill and New 2015, 364). The cluster of children's parts appears as a transgenic organ farm with genitals displayed on humanoid faces. Erected penis-snouts of a-gender pre-puberty kids fashion a dysfunctional wild ornament of this vulgar experiment by means of technological trans-manipulations. According to Dominique Baque, *Zygotic Acceleration* questions the 'formatting' of a society that 'instigates the bodies and eliminates the desires to the benefit of a generalised normalisation behaviours and technological fetishism' (Baque 1998, 73). *Zygotic Acceleration* works as a fantasy about DIY biohacking. It is a blasphemous totem that transgresses sexual normativity through the revival of primal, monstrous practices of body replication.

One of the most striking aspects of biohacking is its assault on the concept of natural law through the technological reinvention of life forms, something that *Zygotic Acceleration* expresses poignantly with the radically playful randomness of the Chapmans' biotech children. This technological distancing from the essentialism of nature, embodied by *Zygotic Acceleration*, spawns uncanny progeny beyond any obvious form of sexuality. Mobilising the imagination of genetic engineering and cloning, it also flirts with the fetishist 'theatrical exercise' (Byrne 2013, 7) of sadomasochism. The latter has been described by Romana Byrne as a vivid form of what she considers 'aesthetic sexuality', a practice which eludes the concepts of natural laws and 'resists an essentialised ontology of sexuality' (Byrne 2013, 7) by playing with the possibility of reinventing sexual performance. Byrne analyses sadomasochism historically as a cultural practice that produces new forms of desire through the detachment of the aesthetic forms of sexual performance from reproduction. In this sense the theatre of pleasure becomes 'desexualised' in the process of the creation of new forms of pleasure, 'enabled by shifting attention from the genitals to the entire body' (Byrne 2013, 8), which for Byrne is symptomatic not only of sadomasochism but also of all queer sex. SM in her view taps into natural desires, albeit it 'paradoxically requires cultivation' (15) to achieve its forms of erotic art of 'performing or play-acting power dynamics' (129).

In Byrne's articulation, sadomasochism not only abandons sexual reproductive functions by means of historically developing cultural practice, but is also linked to the development of industrial technology. In her conclusion, Byrne suggests a dialogue between the 'history of sadomasochism, a particular form of sexual subjectivity, and the history of aesthetic philosophy' (159). With the beginning of the industrial revolution in the late 18th century aesthetics was developed as a complex philosophy of mind, in parallel to the high technological relationship of humans with nature, which began to emerge then – while also constructing this very idea of nature. At the same time sadomasochism develops in Western culture as a sophisticated practice of artificial sexuality. Byrne stresses the point that although SM and other forms of fetishism may reference some ideas of a natural drive, they are nevertheless always defined against sexual essentialism, as the development of the practice requires an obsessive training of sensitivity. They are practical arts of creating unique forms of pleasure through elaborate post-sexual performances, which converge with the technological pursuit of genetic engineering and other biomediatic practices. Sadomasochists and biopunks share their indulgence in the beyond-sexual recreation of the human body 'through sublime self-dissolution and reconstitution' (Byrne 2013, 161) of performative self-fashioning.

Realising that 'since first congealing in the primordial ooze billions of years ago, DNA has spent all but an infinitesimal slice of the earth's history reproducing itself on its own schedule and in own combinations' (Wohlsen 2011, 55), biopunks want to be the beginning of the new technological trend of widely accessible DNA engineering. 'As reading and writing DNA becomes more and more like processing bits and bytes, the closer genetics comes to being a part of everyday life' (Wohlsen 2011, 121), they claim and perform yet another variant of the fungosexual reproduction of their bodies through media. Since DNA synthesis companies have been in operation for a while, biotech becomes as 'natural' as it is 'to take the basic stuff of our organic existence and add it to your online shopping cart' (Wohlsen 2011, 143). The Internet opens up direct access to the transhuman body through that process. The screens of networked computers outside of human bodies function as interiors of their cells, as they allow biopunks to monitor and manipulate the miniscule movements of their lives. This relationship makes some of the people playing with biopunk activism negate the demarcation between the inside and the outside of the techno-human media-body. One of them is Philip Ross, a bioartist from the San Francisco area, who directly links the above-described phenomena with fungi in his project *Mycotecture*. Mushrooms Reishi or Ling-Chi are the raw materials of his sculptures 'as they grow up within wooden frames to form tall, sturdy arches and walls' (Wohlsen 2011, 202). Traditional mushroom breeding techniques play a similar role to genetic engineering in the shaping of living organisms for humans. In this project, fungi are formed into strong and durable bricks for DIY architectural recombinations. They can also be used to make mushroom tea but, more importantly, they can sensitise humans to a more subtle perception of life through the processes of decomposition, thus transgressing any utilitarian function of myco-tech. In his aesthetic masterpiece *In the Praise of Shadows*, Jun'ichiro Tanizaki accentuates the Eastern appreciation of decomposition as the most refined form of perception. He concludes that 'if indeed "elegance is frigid", it can as well be described as filthy' (Tanizaki

1977, 11). An aesthetic study of decomposition thus seems to offer a gateway to the reimagining of humans, who are invited by Tanizaki to learn their future from dirt.

The *Mycotecture* project involves the imagination of biopunks but without using the tools of genetic engineering. It brings to our attention the fleshy presence of porous membranes that actually perform the body, beyond any reductionist scenarios of DNA code determinism. In my fungi media narration, I desire to spectacularly expose the glands that secrete DNA mixtures, regardless of the mathematical abstraction of the genetic code. Mishima, a cult writer and butoh dance collaborator of Hijikata, suggested that words should 'cut (the) flesh away' (Appignanesi 2002, 336) to expose that the 'mind stinks in (the) guts, like a sewer' (Appignanesi 2002, 339). Mishima's literary method explores the dark vitalism of human communication and body media. In his literature, Mishima gives an account of the medium of writing and its resonance with his body. As his writing penetrates human bodies beyond rational calculations, it performs 'irrational encounters' with live entities within the environment (Sharp and Graham 2015). The bodies of fungi and slime moulds reveal the unsettling vitalism of biology, as they animate decay or creep, radically transgressing the integrity of the human body. In that sense they capture the hypnotic attraction of media indulgence. Their shapes and moves are strangely reminiscent of the new aesthetic endeavours of the queer art of bodily manipulations online – and of post-Internet mutant performance.

The Humus of Holobiont and Queer Rot

Performing post-Internet acts with microbial bodies at the Dungeons of Polymorphous Pan has been philosophically informed by the horizontal approaches to nonhuman materialities. My embodiment of those approaches is revealed in the ongoing biomedia project *Holobiont* [fig. 26]. The term 'holobiont' originally described the evolution of life through the mutation of the entanglement of many species that come together as living networks, as explained by Lynn Margulis (Margulis 2001). I understand this term as an expression of the queer relationship of human performers' bodies to the performance of microbes' bodily entities. Inspired by Donna Haraway (Haraway 2008), I understand 'queer' not only as a non-normative form of human sexuality but also as an expression of a transhuman intimacy with other life forms. In this understanding queer also signals a desire associated with the mutant possibilities of a future life. For the *Holobiont* project I used my film footage of restrained body parts, fragmenting them and turning them into abstract landscapes of flesh by means of video editing. I then projected the fleshy video entities on the living microbial entities that were feeding on rotten materials in the Dungeons. These hybrid biomedia thus performed as queer relations between humans and microbes.

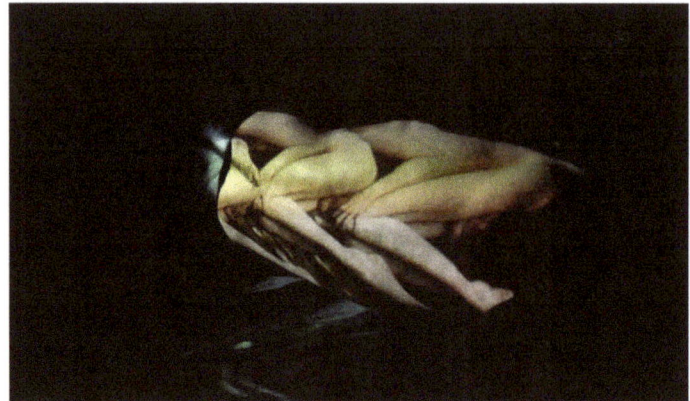

Fig. 26. Loi Wang, 2017. *Holobiont* video projection on the body of Piotr Bockowski. Image courtesy of the artist.

The root of the English word *queer* means *spoil*, *ruin* or *wreck* and this spectrum of meanings is what I capture in my 'fungosexual' analysis of performative bodily mutations. Speculating on the theories of non-normative sexualities, Zach Blas (Blas 2012, 107) considers queerness as a form of decay, which he explains in terms of social disengagement. What comes into play is also the creativity of lifestyles that feed on the destruction of social bonds and a decadent *ethics of degeneration*, transgressing the domesticity guarded by family values. Along the same lines, Halberstam recognises in queer sex 'a death drive that undoes the self' (Halberstam 2008, 140). In Halberstam's analysis, the queer subject 'has been bound epistemologically, to negativity, to nonsense, to anti-production, to unintelligibility' (Halberstam 2008, 141). The queer body, and particularly that of an effeminate man, is being described as a *self-shattering* body that practices an unwriting, an undoing and an unravelling of the self. Those processes entail for Halberstam negative, masochist and vulnerable acts against oppression, as only a *radical passivity* involved in refusing the system of social control can empower the human. The way it can occur is through the disintegration of individualities, as unified ideas of identity are produced by the control system that conceptualises the humanist self in the first place. Queerness eludes that control through the intensities of decomposing bodies. In this very sense my *Holobiont* is a queer political activity.

Holobiont, like all other mutant performances of the Chronic Illness, engages in a strategy of communication with nonhumans described by Bennett as a 'playful element' (Bennett 2010, 15) in approaching the non-identity of matter. *Holobiont* devolved out of not only rotten materials but also performative gestures of humans that courageously speculate about nonhumans, being aware of not knowing them but still performing with them. Between repeated waves of floods, the Dungeons were exposed during the Chronic Illness events to various modes of performative embodiment of fungi media. They explored narratives of the biomedia devolution of life by means of undoing humans, with the aim to connect them to the bio-forms dispersed through the decaying urban environment.

According to the sociological study *Arrival Cities* (Saunders 2011) by Doug Saunders, at the beginning of the 21st century roughly half of the global population participated in a transition from traditional local farming communities to the hyper-technicised monstrous megalopolises of trans-future. People abandon their traditional localities ruled by strong ties of family structures and dislocate into hyper-diversities of global cities, organised by the network media activity. This phenomenon defines the dwellers by the more dynamic, fluid and fragmentary technological relations to their urban peers as well as the global environments exposed to the greater intensities of the city's impact on them. It calls for new symbiotic transhuman strategies for living, expressed by Haraway in her recent plea, 'Make kin not babies' (Haraway 2016, 5), which calls for the development of human bonds beyond the family, sexuality and other forms of intimate companionship. Haraway postulates a withdrawal from family values and heterosexuality, with a view to seeking kinship with nonhuman life. Considering issues related to overpopulation and the reproduction of social repression mechanisms by family structures, Haraway encourages narrations of human and nonhuman communities coming together through opening up to the sensitivities of coexistence and the intimacies between various life forms. She states that separations of definition of different critters are secondary to the strange intimacies of holobionts that essentially make those critters in a process of their entanglements with each other.

Haraway then goes on to rename humans as 'humus', in an attempt to expand the transhuman intimacies all the way to the most alien forms of life, be they microbial or fungal, embedded in the abiotic matter energies and intensities. 'Plants, along with bacteria and fungi, are also animals' lifelines to communication with the abiotic world, from sun to gas to rock' (Haraway 2016, 122). Opening towards the exploration of transhuman entities that every notion of 'humanity' has to be mediated through, Haraway emphasises the concreteness of the corporeal presence of life. 'Including human people, critters are in each other's presence, or better, inside each other's tubes, folds, and crevices, insides and outsides, and not quite either' (Haraway 2016, 98). Those tubes, folds and crevices emerge before thought and ideas, a statement which urges all theoretical constructs to yet again think through a mutant bodily performance of symbiotic becoming.

The becoming of mutant performers with nonhuman others is related to the general notion of embracing the strangeness of life forms and their worlds as unexpected origins of what can possibly be human. Last but not least, sympoietic becoming falls into the category of queerness as a general metaphysical category. Queer, being a word for the oddity of the other, links with the key notion of the cyborg manifesto. 'Cyborgs are critters in a queer litter .... Queer here means not committed to reproduction of kind and having bumptious relations with futurities' (Haraway 2016, 104). Non-normative sexuality eludes the reproductive function of human sex and deconstructs the social structures based on the traditional family, breeding kin networks that challenge human identity, more than ever in the context of media and urban technologies. Last but not least, there is also a significant 'death drive' diagnosed within technology-inspired odd sexuality, which, as it breeds intensities of excitement, also performs the nourishing processes of fungoid decomposition. As Lyotard commented on distortion aesthetics in art: 'What we are interested in is the dimension of otherness, alteration' (Lyotard 1984, 78). Fascination with disfigurement clearly shows in the techno-perversions of the post-Internet performers of bodily mutations.

3 Decay

Pursuing my exploration of the merging of the communicational understanding of media with the embodiment of media vitalism, I started probing visual parallels between the digital decomposition of an image and organic decay. Attracted by this aesthetic correspondence, I decided to shift my performance practice towards the creation of mutant bodily forms, enacting fungoid and digital reproduction. After years of probing the viscerality of sewage physiology through invasive acts within the microbial entity of urban guts, I conceived a series of alternative experiments. Those experiments were pursued in order to give an account of the technological conditioning of my perception of life, as well as to test how far the correspondence between digital image making and microbial decomposition can go. The experiments were aimed at the digitalisation of my body moving within the alien entity of the rotting space of the Dungeons. The process of digital mediation was undertaken via the 3D scanning of my body parts with a hacked movement detector (produced for a game platform), connected to a laptop. Computer software rendered the images and offered a variety of decomposition modes in the process of editing. The digital decompositions were further merged with photographs of the piles of rot in the Dungeons, and also with my body parts projected onto them [figs. 12-23].

All those forms of remediation interplay with a complex technological performance of moulding multiple photographs of my body into a 3D model that is later rendered into a 2D image and edited together with my macrophotography of fungoids that inhabit the Dungeons. This is to establish the 'aesthetics of telecommunication' (Kac 2005) as defined by Eduardo Kac. This aesthetic mode assigns aesthetic value to the processuality of 'media events' rather than to any 'results' of the actual image composition of my 3D decay. Kac considers communication as the main aesthetic value of media. He also considers 'communication [to be] the essential characteristic of life' (Kac 2005, 218). Following his thinking, I can consider the 3D scanning of fungoids to be a way of participating in their life processes. With a view to this, I 3D-scanned mouldy patterns, rotten materials and fungoid overgrowth within my performance space and meshed it digitally with my own body. The activity became a cyclical process of fungal biotelematics – a form of high-tech communication with nonhumans. High-definition 3D resonances of my gestures dispersed into the amorphous pixel formations, blending with patchy transfigurations of the decomposed Dungeons. The space itself was reconstructed through a computer analysis of the data from the 3D scanner and thus reconfigured, to convey the aesthetics of decomposition via high-tech digital manipulations. The result is the visual convergence of primordial life processes and advanced technological data manipulation. The digital simulation assisted me in the mediatic mergence with the bodily entity of the Dungeons. The mediations also offered a form of kinship with the fungoids, in a similar vein to Annike Flo's 'bioscenography' project 'Cocreat:e:ures', which I got to know only later (Flo 2019a). Flo had spent several months of 2018 inside her basement near Oslo, where she bred fungi companions. She described her experience as 'belonging to another creature. Matter appeared to be dissolving, floating away, including my body – and by proxy also my thoughts. In this tactile world with no clear boundaries between bodies, matter and space I was in the process of becoming less and less defined. As if cells were loosening from my body – one by one joining the particles' (Flo 2019b, 62).

Nano-transmissions have been touching and reacting to the irregular shapes of microbial entities, involving high-definition abstract deformations, which offer a form of coexistence with digital invariants of my own techno-bodily actions. In her hybrid between a tangible and digital environment (as she manipulated the documentation of her fungal environment through computer image editing), Flo not only encountered fungi as potential oddkin but in a way simulated a completely alien life environment of an imaginary planet. Mycelial outer-space expansion performs through darkness, humidity and a multitude of genders of mutable media with the multitude of mushrooming techno-extensions. Those mushrooms are the slimy flesh of cloning architecture of Flo's bioscenography, which consists of spore-secreting tubes and mist. The spore clones replicate the confusing multistructures of mycelial threads and create another unknown hyper-complication of the threading. Visions of environments taken over by alien decay also invite practices of storytelling about transplanetary life infections.Through my technological performances of 3D scanning I attempted to, similarly to Flo, undergo a particular material transformation by 'becoming a medium' (Mitchell 2010, 70) as well as 'move the sense of performance to living matter' (Mitchell 2010, 83), beyond my humanity and towards fungi. This performance was intended as a communication with the mysterious nonhuman entity of the Dungeons of Polymorphous Pan. This entity has been guiding me with aesthetic inspirations for the past few years. Every event, act, rehearsal and body or filming session was a cut into the nonhuman life that had existed there already, before I even entered the space. *3Decay* was thus conceived as a technological platform of shared existence with fungoids.

By shifting the scale of their attention, the mutant performers open up or break apart what previously seemed continuous (Kurtz 1997). In this way, via their media technology the performers step into fungal life and find discrete microspaces for themselves anew, as virtual techno-fungoids. The continuity of the mutant performers' bodies is challenged as the biological fabric reveals itself to be porous. Medical practice and biological sciences examine living bodies but they do not explain their urges to move, to transform – to perform. Technology thus can be said to develop in the history of humans as an evolving metaphor for what our bodies can do or become through the mediation of nonhuman environments.

Simulating alien environments at the Dungeons of Polymorphous Pan, in my bioart experiment with 3D scanning I wanted to engender a different sense of life, one described by Robert Mitchell not as harmony but 'rather [as] a strange, embodied sense of alien, nonorganic life. This is a sense of life as fundamentally excessive, beyond my own goals, intentions, and bodily capacities, and as something that threatens – or promises – to transform even my own agency into media for further transformation' (Mitchell 2010, 89). My e-fungoid body performs microbial behaviour by means of digital technologies. I replicate my selves into entities of bio-digital mutation. By enacting gestures of auto-cannibalism and of the consumption of the technological decomposition of objects, exemplified by the pixel rot of organs, I attempt to replicate technologically through the mediatic mergence with fungal agencies. Here, 3D scanning embodies fungoid mutation via a partial hybrid fusion of my mediated body with the mediated fungoids, a process which connects technological mediation to fungosexual reproduction. Fleshy mutant 'technomorphism' (Baron 2009, 13) fabricates and sculpts bodies of challenged integrity. According to Denis Baron, the art of the technological mutation of the human body works by contemplating the future of the body. Technological mutations often favour reproduction through the dispersion of fragments that merge into ephemeral hybrids. Apparently 'the whole dismantling of the body truly epitomises the symptom of the entrance into a new era' (Baron 2009, 85). Media can thus be said to replicate humans beyond their sexuality, via technological decompositions. In the process, they end up making the no-longer-human bodies fungosexual.

Conclusion

Exploring the philosophical context of mutant performance art, this book has examined – on a theoretical and practical level – some of the ways in which the understanding of the human body is currently being transgressed in bodily mediations unfolding on the Internet. Through critical readings of dark-vitalist philosophies and selected science texts on microbes and fungi, I have argued that these performances allow us to reassess our relationship with microbial and fungoid life. The concept of 'fungi media' has led me to mobilise the generativity of life enacted in fungal processes (processes which are omnipresent, even if they do not consciously register for most people) to think human bodies and the connections between them. Inspired by the digital manipulations of the body image online and its simultaneous disintegration and proliferation through network computing, many performers take those mutant mediations *beyond* the Internet by incorporating them into their transhuman acts. My own performance and curatorial practice at the sewage space of Chronic Illness events has become a laboratory for such acts. Numerous performative remediations of the technological transformations and distortions of human bodies online have taken place at the Chronic Illness space and found new tangible embodiments that embed Internet processes in the organic generativity of fungoid life. My reason for working with ideas *about* (and, in my curatorial and performance practice, with materialities *of*) microbes and fungi springs from a desire to develop a new materialist theory of corporality and sexuality, which I have termed 'fungosexuality', as a way of moving beyond the current concepts of queer and trans theory, and towards the fetishist performance art of the antinatalist affirmation of life.

My reflections on nonhuman life unfold and develop through the aesthetic triggers of mutant performance. I have built a conceptual skeleton for all those performative experiments with body mutations with a view to transgressing the nihilism and commodifying alienation of the body in our present-day media cultures. This approach has been intended to serve as an invitation to practise life-affirming engagement with nonhumans that can take place within, between and around humans. Post-Internet mutant performances marry the decomposition of human bodily forms online with the fertile materialities of fungal decomposition. They open up life-affirming transhuman ecologies beyond the Internet, in a variety of spaces – including that of my own squat which doubles as a performance space. Drawing on Kathy Acker's proposition that 'society is living out its dying in its ruins' (Acker 2018, 63) through urban slum subcultures, I have purposefully examined the post-Internet performance of bodily mutations by situating it in the squatted architecture of decay throughout the duration of my research process (2015-2023). The mediated aesthetics of bodily mutations and the decomposition performance of illness and decay in the context of the collapsing global infrastructures has been orchestrated alongside my writing of this book, in an effort to outline an environmentally-accountable vision of media culture via the fungoid life of human waste.

Looking at the fungal ecologies of the biosphere, mutant performers are seen as joining the ongoing cultural efforts to renegotiate our current understanding of human bodies. Yet mutant performers also create a cultural phenomenon of their own, which, through my curatorial practice involving performance events located within decaying urban infrastructures, I situate within post-industrial subcultures. Through this cross-contamination of philosophy and biology, complemented by my own performance art that attempts to enact some of these ideas, my book aspires to demonstrate that the current subterranean practice involving the digital destruction (or decomposition) of the human body online is not just a macabre fad, or a random throwback to body-horror looks. Mutant performances are a visual, tangible and body-processual form of philosophical reflection on the planetary ecological crisis known as the Anthropocene.

Moving the context of bodily mediation away from disembodied digital forms and into transhuman fungal acts, the phenomenon of mutant performance art opens post-Internet culture to speculative techno-vitalism because it looks at the Internet through the concept (and matter) of microbial intelligence. Post-Internet mutant performers embody this concept in their acts by transferring the image of their online bodily deformation into tangible acts, unfolding within physical performance spaces of decaying metropolitan environments. Curating those practices, processes and spaces over the years has allowed me to develop some corporeal strategies of my own for philosophising about life.

Through my curatorial and performance practice of the Chronic Illness events, I have attempted to enact fungal decomposition as both a biological process and a concept. The Chronic Illness events have allowed me to define the post-Internet bodies of mutant performers not as autonomous individual entities but rather as momenta of the environmental movement of fungoids. I see the performers as being defined by trans-corporeality, as they disperse into perspiration, spray themselves across the space or collapse into porous hollows that absorb the spores of the Dungeons of Polymorphous Pan. From the perspective of the space itself, the Dungeons figuratively consume the bodies of performers and incorporate them into the material amalgams of the Chronic Illness events. This is the environmental, physical mode through which my research has attempted to extend the interrogation of fungoid life beyond traditionally conceived notions of sex and reproduction. In navigating the events, the concept of the 'chronic illness' has allowed me to emphasise the trans-corporeal character of mutant performers as their acts abandon the idea and look of a healthy body. Through what has thus become a form of 'philosophical performance practice' my work aims to actualise a mergence of humanoid bodies with the space of polymorphous Dungeons, with its ongoing fungoid mediation.

The practice of bodily performance unfolding at the Dungeons presented in this book interrogates the fetishism of rot involving queer sexuality as a technologically-mediated polymorphous entanglement between humans and nonhumans. Post-Internet performance has thus become for me an exploration of fantasies pertaining to a trans-species coexistence and coevolution. This exploration has been my way of trying to establish a form of queer sexuality that is not focused on traditional fertility-aiming heterosexual penetration but that rather foregrounds the penetration of posthuman bodies by nonhuman environments, as encapsulated by the fetishism of rot aesthetics. Fungosexuality is not an alternative sexual identity but an alternative mode of bodily replication, turning away from sexual reproduction towards body modifications pertaining to corporeal decomposition fetishes. A growing attraction to monstrous performative mutations is increasingly shared by Internet users who transgress the strictures of the online medium, (re)turning to bodily performance in spaces other than the Internet. In examining how performers enact transhuman body replication beyond human sexual reproduction, my theory of fungosexuality emphasises this fetishist embrace of rot and the desire to transform human bodies into monstrous appearances. In my view, decay fetishism in mutant performance establishes itself as a new way to perpetuate the life of the body. It offers an alternative to conventional human parenting, as performers multiply 'bastardised' versions of their bodies or extend and modify them into creaturely fusions. These practices constitute a post-Internet remediation of the online modifications of human bodies. I also consider them to be a transgression of sexuality that reproduces bodies through performances with fungoids.

The phenomenon of fungosexuality I have proposed in this book embraces a diversifying multitude of non-binary gender identifications. Yet its specificity is captured by an odd choice of pronoun – 'it'. Calling themselves 'it', some mutant performers explicitly reject human individuality related to the status of a person, associating themselves instead with nonhuman life forms. In this way, they allow for the spilling over of their selves into transhuman relations with creatures, substances, material multitudes, environmental processes and chimerical clusters. The 'it' pronoun in the context of my work defines vectors of fungosexual mutations, as the performers focus on connections with nonhuman life forms rather than identity politics.

This alliance with the non-identity of fungoid entities, which I have examined in my book through both philosophy and performance, gains an additional significance in the context of my activity in the squatting movement. Being anonymous, semi-nomadic inhabitants of abandoned architectures who apply anti-surveillance solutions in their lifestyles, squatters are themselves considered a social 'it', as they lack many identity characteristics of regular city dwellers. They join the estimated statistics of 'internally displaced people', who, together with refugees and asylum seekers, amount to over 1% of the world's population. I critically zoom in on that uncertain margin of human living. Displacement is understood here as a violent disruption of one's living conditions related to the lack of shelter. My participation in the squatting movement, which has become the crucial part of my research into fungi media through its location within the transient occupations of decomposing architecture, also offers an example of an 'internal displacement' within urban areas. Looking at this process in the context of the variety of movements of people across history, Robert Cohen presents migration as a major civilisational process and a hybrid human-nonhuman activity – a position I embrace as foundational to mutant performance. 'The flow of people around the world ... is comparable to, and often linked with, the flow of goods, resources, money, images, pollutants, drugs, music, data, and many other aspects of contemporary life,' he says (Cohen 2019, 9). Taking into consideration the 'mobility' perspective has allowed me to interrogate the idea of societies as porous and open-ended processes, with the artistic take on the phenomenon of squatting providing a methodological and conceptual framework for approaching this idea. With this, I have been mindful of the fact that the growing numbers of inhabitants of 21st century megalopolises employ a variety of strategies for their internal displacement. Those strategies arguably offer opportunities for a renegotiation of the dominant ways of life. The mutant performance art of Chronic Illness squatters as presented in my book embraces the context of urban displacement, post-industrial decay and civilisational waste as vital processes that participate in the making of transhuman bodies.

The uprooted identities of squatters become a raw material for the transgressions of mutant performance art. Observing their fungosexual bodily mutations, I have begun to see them as uncoupled from cultural, political and family values, values which serve as foundations for the concepts of human exceptionality in nature and human superiority over other life forms. Mutant performers intentionally transgress these concepts that have led to the industrial exploitation of nonhuman life forms and that have accelerated the extinction of multiple species. To challenge those concepts on the ground of the philosophies of life, I have looked into the micro-scale of civilisational biowaste as the raw material of mutant media performance. The perception of the human's exceptional position amongst other life forms shifts by accentuating the intense changeability of human bodies via their embeddings in the multitude of alien life. Mutant performance art focuses on that very perceptual shift, creating a post-Internet subculture that embraces precarious living within urban decay through acts of life-affirming presence that involve living bodies. The phenomenon of fungosexuality, mapped by the scattered networks of post-Internet mutant performances, involves a number of ethico-aesthetic strategies of investment in decomposition processes, an investment which represents a wider social movement towards the deacceleration of global populations and their industrial societies. I hope that mutant performance art can encourage excitement about the 'deceased beauty' of societal decline, thus curbing so-called development and inspiring the release of technology-trapped energy by observing ecological sustainability, withdrawal from consumerist habits and a decline of sexual reproduction. My conclusion follows a suggestion made by Steve Shaviro that, in the technological environment of overstimulation by media, enforced distraction can be cultivated as a lifestyle choice. The proposed strategy of withdrawal from information overload is manifested by the aesthetics of mutant performers, as they move away from the utilitarian context of computational mediations of the Internet and instead engage in the processes of decomposition by transforming their body shapes.

This book was finished during a major global crisis of infrastructures related to pandemic lockdowns, alongside a series of clandestine theatre events at the

Dungeons of Polymorphous Pan, which, in secrecy, interrogated the narratives of health and biotech power systems lurking behind them. Now, Chronic Illness returns to its vital focus on rot fetishism through commissioning a variety of mutant performance acts curated under the heading of 'Posthuman Pornography'. Currently the event relapses into symptoms of indulgence in the erotic allure of digital rot, biotech cannibalism, vegetative penetration tissues or multi-tubular xeno-genitals rendered into AI video installations, 3D-printed prosthetic pregnancy butoh dance, the psychodrama of systemic sexual exploitation and sewage digestion body art. Importantly, all those modes of performance engage with the fungosexual notion of bodily replication through mutation and fetishism, as opposed to sexual reproduction. This methodology opens up a cultural space for the possibility of diverse subcultures celebrating their vitality through antinatalism. It is driven by the realisation that the acceleration of reproduction and population growth lies at the core of the global environmental and political crisis. The limits of energy sources confronted with multiplying human expansiveness in all dimensions of the biosphere's material organisation cause the overdrive of the post-industrial civilization. This mode of thinking contextualises fungosexuality as a philosophy of life that stands against traditional family values, especially as inscribed in monotheistic religious systems, nation-state or socialist ideologies, as well as other sexually repressive or pro-procreation cultural tribalisms. Here, the Chronic Illness events evoke forms of co-existence that move away from biological procreation and family fatalisms, towards a nomadic focus on life processes. They celebrate decomposition as a more relevant insight into the material conditions of our civilisation, with a view to emerging future global cultures that will marginalise sexual reproduction to engage instead in the rot-fetishism of bodily performance art.

Works Cited

4chan. 2023. https://www.4chan.org/

Abney Park Cemetery. 2023. http://www.abneypark.org/heritage

Acker, Kathy. 2018. *Empire of the Senseless.* New York: Grove Press.

Alaimo, Stacy. 2010. *Bodily Natures.* Bloomington: Indiana University Press.

Amato, Joseph. 2000. *Dust.* Berkeley: University of California Press.

Appignanesi, Richard. 2002. *Yukio Mishima's Report to the Emperor.* London: Sinclar-Stevenson.

Arca. 2017. Interview by Niloufar Haidari. In *Crack*: www.crackmagazine.net/article/long-reads/arca-look-within

Archey, Karen and Robin Peckham. 2014. *Art Post-Internet* booklet. Beijing: Ullens Centre for Contemporary Art.

Artaud, Antonin. 1958. *The Theatre and its Double.* New York, NY: Grove Press.

Artaud, Antonin. 1965. *Anthology*. San Francisco: City Lights Books.

Artaud, Antonin. 1995. *Watchfiends & Rack Screams: Works from the Final Period*. Boston: Exact Change.

Bakaneko, Bonnie. 2019. *Your Body is Not a Temple*. Norwich. www.youtube.com/watch?v=D4CQ_ffXXFU

Ballard, J.G. 1990. *Atrocity Exhibition*. San Francisco: Re: Search.

Ballard, J.G. 1997. *The Drowned World*. London: Indigo.

Baque, Dominique. 1998. *La Photographie Plasticienne*. Paris: Editions du Regard.

Barad, Karen. 2003. 'Posthumanist Performativity: Toward an Understanding of How Matter Comes to Matter'. *Signs*, Vol. 28, No. 3 (Spring): 801-831.

Barad, Karen. 2007. *Meeting the Universe Half Way*. Durham: Duke University Press.

Barad, Karen. 2014. 'Invertebrate Visions: Diffraction of the Brittlestar'. In *Multispecies Salon*. Ed. Eben Kirksey. Durham: Duke University Press.

Barber, Stephen. 2006. *Hijikata: Revolt of the Body*. London: Creation Books.

Barber, Stephen. 2013. *The Anatomy of Cruelty*. London: Sun Vision Press.

Baron, Denis. 2009. *The Mutant Flesh*. Paris: Dis Voir.

Barton, Nicholas. 1992. *The Lost Rivers of London,* London: Historical Publications.

Bauman, Zygmunt. 2000. *Liquid Modernity.* Cambridge: Polity Press.

Bauman, Zygmunt. 2004. *Wasted Lives.* Cambridge: Polity Press.

Bellmer, Hans. 2005. *The Doll.* London: Atlas Press.

Bennett, Jane. 2010. *Vibrant Matter.* Durham: Duke University Press.

Blas, Zach. 2012. 'Queerness, Openness'. In *Leper Creativity.* Eds. Edward Keller, Nicola Masciandaro and Eugene Thacker. NYC: punctum books.

Bolender, Karen. 2014. 'R.A.W. Assmilk Soap'. In *Multispecies Salon.* Ed. Eben Kirksey. Durham: Duke University Press.

Bolter, Jay David and Richard Grusin. 2000. *Remediation: Understanding New Media,* Cambridge: MIT Press.

Braidotti, Rosi. 2019. 'A Theoretical Framework for the Critical Posthumanities'. *Theory, Culture & Society,* Vol. 36(6): 31-61.

Brassier, Ray and Robin McKay. 2012. Editors' Introduction. In: Ray Brassier and Robin McKay (eds), *Fanged Noumena,* Falmouth: Urbanomic.

Bridle, James. 2011. *The New Aesthetic.* https://jamesbridle.com/works/the-new-aesthetic

Burroughs, William. 1990. Preface to *Atrocity Exhibition*. In *Re: Search*. San Francisco: Re: Search.

Burroughs, William. 1992. *Soft Machine*. London: Groove Press.

Butler, Judith. 1990. *Gender Trouble: Feminism and the Subversion of Identity*. New York and London: Routledge.

Byrne, Roman. 2013. *Aesthetic Sexuality: A Literary History of Sadomasochism*. New York: Bloomsbury.

Catts, Oron and Ionat Zurr. 2002. 'Growing Semi-Living Sculptures'. *Leonardo*, Vol.35, No.4.

CCRU. 2017. *Writings 1997-2003*. Falmouth: Urbanomics.

Chronic Illness. 2023. http://neofung.tumblr.com/chronicillness

Cioran, E.M. 1975. *A Short History of Decay*. Oxford: Basil Blackwell.

Cohen, Robyn. 2019. *Migration*. London: Andre Deutsch.

Colebrook, Claire. 2008. 'On Not Becoming Man: The Materialist Politics of Unactualised Potential'. In *Material Feminisms*. Eds. Alaimo Stacy and Susan Hekman. Bloomington: Indiana University Press.

Coleman, Beth. 2011. *Hello Avatar*. Cambridge, MA: MIT Press.

Crooked, Emily. 2019. 'How this artist is challenging conservatism in Brazilian political rhetoric', *Daze Digital*, 11 January, https://www.dazeddigital.com/beauty/soul/article/42849/1/artist-body-rhetoric-brazilian-politics

Darwin, Charles. 1861. *On the Origin of Species*. New York: D. Appleton and Company.

Deleuze, Gilles and Felix Guattari. 1983. *Anti-Oedipus: Capitalism and Schizophrenia*, Minneapolis: University of Minnesota Press.

Flo, Annike. 2019a. 'Concreat:e:ures'. In *Carry the Fire zine 001*. Carry the Fire: London.

Flo, Annike. 2019b. Interview by Tina Gorjanc, *CLOT* (24 July), https://clotmag.com/interviews/annike-flo-scenographic-perspectives-of-the-anthropocene

Fortenberry, Diane, Rebecca Morrill and Josephine New. 2015. *The Body of Art*. London: Phaidon.

Freud, Sigmund. 1919. *Totem and Taboo*. London: Routledge & Sons.

Freud, Sigmund. 1920. 'The Infantile Sexuality' in: *Three Contributions to the Theory of Sex*. New York and Washington: Nervous and Mental Disease Publishing Co. Available on Wikisource.

Freud, Sigmund. 2002. *The Schreber Case*. London: Penguin.

Garner, Stanton B. Jr. 2006. 'Artaud, Germ Theory, and the Theatre of Contagion'. Theatre Journal Vol. 58, No. 1 (March): 1-14.

Gasparini, Gabriella. 2018. 'Beauty Uncut'. *Judas Magazine* #4, London.

Gibson, William. 1984. *Neuromancer*. New York: ACE.

Griggs, Claudine. 1998. S/he. *Changing Sex and Changing Clothes*. Oxford: Berg.

Halberstam, Judith. 2008. 'The Anti-Social Turn in Queer Studies'. *Graduate Journal of Social Science* Vol. 5 Issue 2. Tel Aviv.

Haraway, Donna. 1991. *Simians, Cyborgs and Women: The Reinvention of Nature*. New York: Routledge.

Haraway, Donna. 2008. *When Species Meet*. Minneapolis: University of Minnesota Press.

Haraway, Donna. 2016. *Staying with the Trouble: Making Kin in the Chthulucene*. Durham: Duke University Press.

Heim, Michael. 1993. *The Metaphysics of Virtual Reality*. New York: Oxford University Press.

Hendriks, Martijn and Katja Novitskova. 2014. 'Post-Internet Materialism'. In: *Metropolis Magazine*. 6 June, http://www.metropolism.com/en/features/23573_post_internet_materialism

Hertz, Garnet and Jussi Parikka. 2012. 'Zombie Media: Circuit Bending Media Archeology into an Art Method'. *Leonardo*, Vol. 45, No 5: 424-430.

Hird, Myra J. 2004. 'Naturally Queer'. *Feminist Theory* Vol.5, No.1.

Hird, Myra J. 2017. 'Proliferation, Extinction, and an Anthropocene Aesthetic'. In *Posthumous Life*. Eds Claire Colebrook and Jami Weinstein. New York: Columbia University Press.

Hooke, Robert. 1665. *Micrographia: or, Some Physiological Descriptions of Minute Bodies Made by Magnifying Glasses. With Observations and Inquiries Thereupon.* London: J. Martyn. (online https://digital.sciencehistory.org/works/xw42n912b)

Ihde, Don. 2002. *Bodies in Technology.* Minneapolis: University of Minneapolis Press.

Institution of Rot. 2023. www.youtube.com/nerval45/about

Kac, Eduardo. 2005. *Telepresence and Bio Art.* Detroit: University of Michigan Press.

Kafka, Franz. 1961. *Parables and Paradoxes.* New York: Schocken Books.

Kahn, Douglas. 1999. *Noise Water Meat.* Cambridge, MA: MIT Press.

Kember, Sarah and Joanna Zylinska. 2012. *Life After New Media.* Cambridge, MA: MIT Press.

Kholeif, Omar. Ed. 2014. *You Are Here: Art After the Internet.* Manchester: HOME Publications.

Kirksey, Eben, Brandon Castelloe-Kuehn and Dorion Sagan. 2014. 'Life in the Age of Biotechnology'. In *Multispecies Salon*. Ed. Eben Kirksey. Durham: Duke University Press.

Kroker, Arthur. 2012. *Body Drift*. Minneapolis: University of Minnesota Press.

Kurtz, Glenn. 1997. 'The Aesthetics of Scale', http://www.glennkurtz.com/cgi-bin/iowa/essays/aesthetics/index.html [now unavailable]

Kurzweil, Ray. 2013. 'Progress and Relinquishment'. In *The Transhumanist Reader: Classical and Contemporary Essays on the Science, Technology, and Philosophy of the Human Future*. Eds. Max More and Natasha Vita-More. Chichester: Wiley-Blackwell.

Land, Nick and Sadie Plant. 1994. 'Cyberpositive'. In *Unnatural: Techno-Theory for a Contaminated Culture*. Ed. Matthew Fuller. London: Underground.

Land, Nick. 2011. *Fanged Noumena*. London: Urbanomics.

Latour, Bruno. 1999. *Pandora's Hope*. Cambridge, MA: Harvard University Press.

Latour, Bruno. 2015. 'Some Experiments in Art and Politics'. *e-flux journal: The Internet Does Not Exist*. Berlin: Sternberg Press.

Lee, Kihan. 2006. 'Embodiment/Disembodiment Dichotomy in William Gibson's Neuromancer'. *Journal of British and American Studies* No. 14 https://pdfs.semanticscholar.org/086b/6692714c8a0a926704ed179b45e795e238cb.pdf

Lovink, Geert. 2016. *Social Media Abyss*. Cambridge: Polity.

Lyotard, Jean-François. 1978. 'Notes on the Critical Function of the Work of Art'. In *Driftworks*. Ed. Roger McKeon. New York: Semiotext(e).

Mackay, Robin. 2012. 'Brief History of Geotrauma'. In *Leper Creativity*. Eds. Edward Keller, Nicola Masciandaro and Eugene Thacker. NYC: punctum books.

MacKenzie, Gordene Olga. 1994. *Transgender Nation*. Bowling Green: Bowling Green State University Popular Press.

Margulis, Lynn and Dorion Sagan. 2000. *What Is Life?* Berkeley: University of California Press.

Margulis, Lynn. 2001. *The Symbiotic Planet*. London: Phoenix.

Mauries, Patrick. 2017. *Androgyne*. London: Thames & Hudson.

McLuhan, Marshall. 2001. *Understanding Media: The Extensions of Man*. London: Routledge.

Mitchell, Robert. 2010. *Bioart and the Vitality of Media*. Seattle: University of Washington Press.

More, Max and Natasha Vita-More. Eds. 2013. *The Transhumanist Reader: Classical and Contemporary Essays on the Science, Technology, and Philosophy of the Human Future*. Chichester: Wiley-Blackwell.

Morton, Timothy. 2017. *Humankind*. London and New York: Verso.

Negarestani, Reza. 2008. *Cyclonopedia: Complicity with Anonymous Materials*. Melbourne: re.press.

Negarestani, Reza. 2014. *Symposium: Speculations on Anonymous Materials*. Fridericanium Kassel. 18 January, https://www.youtube.com/watch?v=FgolMebGt9I

Newman, Lisa. 2010. 'Flesh for Fantasy: The future of sado-masochism and performance art in virtual worlds', https://www.academia.edu/5593267/Flesh_for_fantasy_The_future_o_sado-masochism_and_performance_art_in_the_virtual_world?email_work_card=interaction_paper

Officina Corpuscoli. 2023. https://www.corpuscoli.com/

ORLAN. 1990. *Surgery Performance*. http://www.orlan.eu/portfolio/first-surgery-performance-paris-july-1990/

Paasonen, Susanna. 2011. *Carnal Resonance*. Cambridge, MA: MIT Press.

Paglia, Camille. 1991. *Sexual Personae*. New York: Vintage Books.

Parma Ham. 2019. https://www.parmaham.tv/nullo

Paxons, Heather. 2014. *'Microbiopolitics'*. In *Multispecies Salon*. Ed. Eben Kirksey. Durham: Duke University Press.

Peters, John Durham. 2015. *The Marvelous Clouds: Toward a Philosophy of Elemental Media*. Chicago: University of Chicago Press.

Petridis, Alexis. 2017. 'How cruising, graveyards and swan songs inspired Arca's new album', *The Guardian*, 6 April, https://www.theguardian.com/music/2017/apr/06arca-new-album-alejandro-ghersi-kanye-west-bjork

P-Orridge, Genesis. 2006a. *Pandrogeny Manifesto* Part 1 https://www.youtube.com/watch?v=82Y9oGxBVV0

P-Orridge, Genesis. 2006b. *Pandrogeny Manifesto* Part 2 https://www.youtube.com/watch?v=DkhCkSXbYaE

P-Orridge, Genesis. 2021. *Nonbinary*. New York: Abrams Press.

Reed, Jeremy. 2006. 'Heliogabalus: Black Sun Rising'. In *Caligula: Divine Carnage*. Eds. Stephen Barber and Jeremy Reed. London: Solar Books.

Rodriguez, Juan Carlos. 2018. 'Towards a Film Mycology?'. *Public Journal*, No.57. Toronto.

Royle, Nicholas. 2003. *The Uncanny*. Manchester: Manchester University Press.

Rubel, Dietmar. 2012. 'Plasticity: An Art History of the Mutable'. In *Materiality*. Ed. Petra Launge-Berndt. London: Whitechapel Gallery and MIT Press.

Ryan, Frank. 2009. *Virolution*. London: Collins.

Saunders, Doug. 2011. *Arrival Cities*. London: Windmill Books.

Seymour, Nicole. 2019. *Bad Environmentalism: Irony and Irrelevance in the Ecological Age*. Minneapolis: University of Minnesota Press.

Sharp, Jasper and Tim Graham. 2015. *The Creeping Garden: Irrational Encounters with Plasmodia Slime Moulds*. Godalming: Alchimia.

Simun, Miriam. 2014. 'Human Milk'. In *Multispecies Salon*. Ed. Eben Kirksey. Durham: Duke University Press.

Sloterdijk, Peter. 2011. *Bubbles*. Cambridge, MA: MIT Press.

Sontag, Susan. 1977. *Illness as Metaphor*. New York: Farrar, Straus and Giroux.

Stamets, Paul. 2005. *Mycelium Running*. Berkeley: Ten Speed Press.

Stengers, Isabelle. 2015. *In Catastrophic Times: Resisting the Coming Barbarism*. London and Lueneburg: Open Humanities Press and Meson Press.

Steyerl, Hito. 2015. 'Too Much World: Is the Internet Dead?'. *e-flux journal: The Internet Does Not Exist*. Berlin: Sternberg Press.

Strugatsky, Arkady and Boris. 2007. *Roadside Picnic*. London: Gollancz.

Szerszynski, Bronislaw. 2003. 'Technology, Performance and Life Itself: Hannah Arendt and the Fate of Nature'. In *Nature Performed*. Eds. Bronislaw Szerszynski, Claire Waterton and Wallace Heim. Oxford: Blackwell Publishing.

Tanizaki, Jun'ichiro. 1977. *In the Praise of Shadows*. Stony Creek: Leete's Island Books.

Thacker, Eugene. 2004. *Biomedia*. Minneapolis: University of Minnesota Press.

Thacker, Eugene. 2010. *In the Dust of this Planet*. Winchester: Zero Books.

Thacker, Eugene. 2018. 'Foreword'. In *Death, Mort, Tod. A European Book of the Dead*. Eds. Steve Finbow and Karolina Urbaniak. London: Infinity Land Press.

The Dungeons of Polymorphous Pan archive: https://neofung.tumblr.com/chronicillness

Trewavas, Anthony. 2014. *Plant Behaviour and Intelligence*. Oxford: Oxford University Press.

Tsing, Anna. 2015. *The Mushroom at the End of the World*. Princeton: Princeton University Press.

Varela, Francisco J. 1991. *The Embodied Mind*. Cambridge, MA: MIT Press.

Vasudevan, Alexander. 2017. *The Autonomous City*. New York: Verso.

Vecchi, Benedetto. 2004. 'Introduction' to Zygmunt Bauman, *Identity*. Cambridge: Polity Press.

Virilio, Paul and Sylvère Lotringer. 2002. *Corpuscular Dawn*. Los Angeles: Semiotext(e).

Virilio, Paul. 2000. *Information Bomb*. London: Verso.

Virilio, Paul. 2006. *Art and Fear*. London: Continuum.

Volk, Tyler. 2003. *Gaia's Body: Toward a Physiology of Earth*. Cambridge, MA: MIT Press.

Weinreb, Ben and Christopher Hibbert. Eds. 1983. *The London Encyclopaedia*. London: MacMillan.

Wohlsen, Marcus. 2011. *Biopunk*. New York: Current.

Woodard, Ben. 2012a. *Slime Dynamics*. Winchester: Zero Books.

Woodard, Ben. 2012b. 'The Untimely (and Unshapely) Decomposition of Onto-Epistemological Solidity: Negarestani's *Cyclonopedia* as Metaphysics'. In *Leper Creativity*. Eds. Edward Keller, Nicola Masciandaro and Eugene Thacker. NYC: punctum books.

Woodard, Ben. 2013. *On an Ungrouded Earth*. NYC: punctum books.

Woodard, Ben. 2017. 'Disinternment Loops'. *Cyclopes Journal*. No.2, Amsterdam, https://www.cyclopsjournal.net/

Zerzan, John. 1994. *Future Primitive*. Columbia: Autonomedia & Anarchy.

Žižek, Slavoj. 2004. *Organs without Bodies*. New York: Routledge.

Zylinska, Joanna. 2014. *Minimal Ethics for the Anthropocene.* Ann Arbor: Open Humanities Press.

www.ingramcontent.com/pod-product-compliance
Lightning Source LLC
Chambersburg PA
CBHW041920240526
45473CB00039B/2924